Kirkpatrick Then and Now:
A Strong Foundation For the
Future

Kirkpatrick Then and Now: A Strong Foundation For the Future

James D. Kirkpatrick, Ph.D.

Wendy Kayser Kirkpatrick

Kirkpatrick Partners, LLC
124 N. Rock Hill Road
Saint Louis, MO 63119
(314) 961-4848
information@kirkpatrickpartners.com
kirkpatrickpartners.com

The following marks are the property of Kirkpatrick Partners, LLC:

The Kirkpatrick Business Partnership Model[SM]
KBPM[SM]
Return on Expectations[SM]
ROE[SM]
Chain of Evidence[SM]

ISBN 978-1-44867-059-8

We dedicate this book to our fathers, Don Kirkpatrick and John Kayser.

Don, for his tremendous contribution to the world of workplace learning and performance, and for inspiring us to carry on his work in everything we do.

John, for being Wendy's voice of encouragement and telling her to always believe in herself.
While he isn't with us anymore, we know that he is looking down with pride on his daughter's first published book.

Thank you for making this book possible in your own unique ways.

Contents

Foreword

So long as an expert has existed and an apprentice was willing, training and development has been an integral and necessary part of human evolution. Over time, the formality of the process has been enhanced and improved; methodologies for training have capitalized on style, preferences, capabilities and technologies.

In 1959 the genesis of a practical methodology for evaluating training and development was conceived and has become the cornerstone for all Training and Development professionals who understand the need for feedback to assess the success and impact of a program as well as to enhance and improve its ability to meet expectations. A multi-leveled approach to review how well the program was achieving it's objectives across a range of feedback points that ultimately informs everyone in the process, the designer, developer, implementer, investor, and student, created a firm platform for continuous improvement of the work.

The four levels of training evaluation have become ubiquitous and interconnected with all endeavors focused on training. So much so that sometimes we forget the overall connection as it has become integral to the process as part of a cohesive and comprehensive model for training development. Through the course of program development, I often talk to colleagues, both tenured and new to our vocation, about the Kirkpatrick Model and how they may leverage it for their training programs; often to an interesting reaction, "Kirkpatrick Model?" As I share my thoughts on the importance of evaluation to understand how well the program is doing or how it may be improved, the reaction is always the same, the four levels of evaluation...of course it's part of the process, and fully integrated into the program, without a second thought! The process and structure have transcended the test of time. It's safe to say that all trainers ask for the "smile-sheet" –the reaction to a training program. And, with each level of evaluation building upon the other, it provides a structure and process to assess the success, or opportunity for improvement, of any training program. More importantly, the structured methodology for assessing training introduced by Donald Kirkpatrick provides for a practical and repeatable process allowing us to compare success across our programs to create a platform for use of best practices as we build new or improve existing training.

In every profession there are heroes and stars. Some are more recognizable than others; people in sports, political office, or those who have gained noteworthiness through other endeavors. In the world of training and development we have few...Donald Kirkpatrick is certainly one of those heroes.

Vince Gonzalez
Training and Development
Booz Allen Hamilton

Preface

Understanding a model is nothing like knowing the person behind it. This book is as much about Don Kirkpatrick and his contribution to the field of workplace learning and development as it is about the Kirkpatrick Four Level Evaluation Model. As true ambassadors of Don's work and the updates and additions herein, we know that the four levels are more than just four practical words that constitute the long-standing, industry standard for program evaluation.

To honor Don's work and the deeper intentions of it, we first dedicate this book to Don. In it, you will read about how he came to coin the four words, what the major premises have been and continue to be, and how we are all evolving the model to better meet the challenges of our business stakeholders.

We also want to honor and thank those who, over the past 50 years, have taken Don's work and sharpened, tweaked, applied, researched, and championed it. Many of you continue to work closely with us as we find new applications and opportunities to leverage old truths, and we greatly appreciate each and every one of you.

At the end of 50 years, there still exist many misconceptions about what the four levels are, and what Don intended by them. We take this opportunity to clarify and expand the model in the clearest terms we can. We trust the new, fresh version of the model presented here will answer most of the questions and allay the apprehensions you have had about the actual application of the four levels. Foremost, we want you to hear the message that the ultimate intent of this model is to maximize training effectiveness as defined not from our perspective, but from the perspectives of our business partners – our ultimate customers.

The bottom line is that we salute Don, and do our best in our work every day to bring his true model to life.

We hope that you read this book with the intention of improving your application of the Kirkpatrick Four Levels – reaction, learning, behavior, and results. More so, we want you to become *ambassadors* – not of the Kirkpatricks – but of the principles and the potential to bring untold value to the business, its customers and employees.

There are many people we want to thank for helping us with this project. First and foremost, Don himself. And Fern, his wife of 59 years, who undoubtedly helped all of this to happen! Mark Morrow at ASTD for unearthing the original four articles from 1959 and 1960. Vince Gonzalez, for the foreword. Dave Basarab and Jack Phillips, for their historical accounts. We also thank those who provided their kind words and accolades to Don: Elaine Biech, Svetlana Chumakova, Stephen R. Covey, Rollin Glaser, Judith Hale, Ronald Meyer, Susan Muehlbach, R. Palan, Germán A. París, Bob Pike, Al Thomas, and Michael Woodard. Finally, we thank the people who helped with the physical assembly of our first self-published title: Cindy Anderson and Debbie Elmer. We could not have done this project without the personal contributions of each of you!

Jim and Wendy Kirkpatrick

Introduction

When you read this book that my son, Jim, and his wife, Wendy have written, you will realize that I have nothing to add but the four levels. I would like to thank them for the work they have done in creating this 50-year memory.

I would also like to thank the people who have helped to make the four levels known and useful. These are the many professionals, too numerous to mention by name, who made presentations and/or wrote case studies for our books describing the ways to implement the levels.

Finally, I want to thank my wife Fern for encouraging and supporting me during the many hours and days I spent developing and teaching the four levels. I am sure she knows almost as much about the four levels as I do.

I hope that you find this book not only interesting, but also helpful in your future evaluation efforts.

Don Kirkpatrick, Ph.D.

THEN: THE KIRKPATRICK FOUR LEVELS

This section of the book is dedicated to the history of the Kirkpatrick Four Levels: what transpired between 1959 and 2009.

When terming this section "then", in no way does this imply that these principles are antiquated or no longer of value. Quite the opposite. We include this section to share the strong foundation upon which The Kirkpatrick Model is built.

We are often asked how the Four Levels came to be. Don Kirkpatrick answers that question in his own words in chapter two. There are also excerpts from his Ph.D. dissertation.

This section includes the original four articles published in the *Journal of the American Society of Training Directors* (now known as *T+D Magazine*). The articles are presented in their original, unedited form. Keep in mind that at the time, training professionals were exclusively male, language usage was different, and typesetting and layout capabilities were not what they are today. We hope you enjoy this peek at the *true* historical content!

We wrap up with section with notes of congratulations from Don's contemporaries, and key contributors to the world of workplace learning and business education.

Chapter 1

ഔഃ

The Kirkpatrick Four Levels

For those of you who are not already familiar with the Kirkpatrick Four Levels, here is a brief overview.

Level 1: Reaction	To what degree participants react favorably to the learning event.
Level 2: Learning	To what degree participants acquire the intended knowledge, skills, and attitudes based on their participation in the learning event.
Level 3: Behavior	To what degree participants apply what they learned during training when they are back on the job.
Level 4: Results	To what degree targeted outcomes occur as a result of the learning event(s) and subsequent reinforcement.

LEVEL 1: REACTION

> **Reaction:** To what degree participants react favorably to the learning event.

As the word *reaction* implies, evaluation at this level measures how those who participate in a program react to it. Don Kirkpatrick also calls it a measure of customer satisfaction. Don feels that measuring reaction is important for both public and in-house programs. In the case of public programs, organizations paid a fee to send their associates to the class. Reaction has to be favorable if the training organization is to attract new customers, have repeat and referral clients, and stay in business.

It isn't quite as obvious that reaction to in-house programs is also important. In some cases, participants are required to attend whether they want to or not. However, they are still "customers" even if they don't pay, or even choose the program they attend. Their reactions can make or break a training program. What they say to their bosses after attending often gets to higher-level managers, who make decisions about the future of training programs. So positive reactions are just as important for in-house as public programs.

It is important to get a positive reaction in most cases for the viability of the training program. In addition, there is a high correlation between Level 1 Reaction scores and learning. Positive reaction may not ensure learning, but negative reaction almost certainly reduces the possibility of it occurring.

Level 1 is most commonly measured with a written reaction sheet or survey near the end of a program. It can also be measured later with a survey, interview, or focus group to get participant reactions after some time has passed.

LEVEL 2: LEARNING

> **Learning:** To what degree participants acquire the intended knowledge, skills, and attitudes based on their participation in the learning event.

From this definition, increase in knowledge, increase in skill, and change in attitude are the three things that a training program can accomplish. Programs dealing with topics like diversity in the workforce aim primarily at changing attitudes. Technical programs, like how to use a computer program, aim at improving skills. Programs on topics like leadership, motivation, and communication can aim at all three objectives. In order to evaluate learning, the specific objectives must be determined.

When Learning Has Taken Place

1. Knowledge is increased

2. Skill is improved

3. Attitudes are changed

Knowledge can be measured with written tests, demonstrations, role-plays, and other activities during the training class. Skills are best measured with simulations, hands-on demonstrations, and other close approximations to the actual activity. Attitudes can be measured with verbal or written questions and interviews during the class.

As with reaction, learning does not need to be measured only during or immediately following the class. A delayed measurement may be conducted with a quiz or skills demonstration at some point after the class has been completed.

LEVEL 3: BEHAVIOR

> **Behavior**: To what degree participants apply what they learned during training when they are back on the job.

In simple terms, Behavior measures to what degree training graduates are doing what they are supposed to be doing on the job in order to bring about the desired Level 4 Results. In some instances, it will be important to determine the *change in behavior* following the learning event. This requires the use of pre and post-assessments, unless it can be determined that the content is totally new to all of the participants.

Studies show that relatively few programs get measured beyond Level 2. This is unfortunate, because learning in and of itself is of little value if the training participant does not apply the information by doing something differently back on the job. This means that Level 3 is absolutely critical to monitor and measure for a training initiative to have value.

Measuring Level 3 does not have to be difficult. It does, however, usually require the managers and supervisors as partners in the effort. Level 3 Behaviors are exhibited when training participants are back on the job and no longer being observed by the training professional. So managers and supervisors often serve as the "eyes and ears" to validate if the trainees have adopted the desired behaviors that were taught in class. Since Level 3 moves outside of the direct control of the workplace learning professional, we often call the space between Level 2 and Level 3 "the great divide."

It is important for workplace learning professionals to know what type of climate participants will face when they return from the training program. It is also important for them to do everything they can to ensure that the climate will support, encourage, and reward the desired behaviors. Otherwise there is little chance that the training program will accomplish the behavior and results objectives; participants may not even try to use what they have learned. If no change occurs, training participants may be frustrated because they took time to attend training for knowledge and skills they are unable to apply on the job.

Level 3 can be measured through observation, surveys, work reviews, focus groups, and interviews.

LEVEL 4: RESULTS

> **Results**: To what degree targeted outcomes occur as a result of the learning event(s) and subsequent reinforcement.

Results are simply the final outcomes that occur in whole or in part because the participants have attended a program and applied what they learned.

Examples of Typical Results Organizations Seek

- Increased production
- Increased sales
- Improved quality
- Reduced turnover
- Decreased costs
- Higher profits
- Reduced frequency and / or severity of accidents

It is important to recognize that results like these are the reason for having most training programs. Therefore, the final objectives of the training program need to be stated in these terms. If the overall objective of a training program is stated in terms of learning, this should be reviewed to ensure that the course will actually contribute to an organizational-level result.

Some results are intangible, like increased customer satisfaction, intellectual capital, and employee morale. These measures can be just as important as the more tangible examples, but are hard to measure on their own. In the case of these intangibles, it is best to connect them to a corresponding tangible measurement for feasibility and credibility in the evaluation process. For example, if your goal is to increase customer satisfaction, perhaps there is a link to increased sales, better customer retention, or higher scores on a customer service survey.

We typically suggest that Level 4 is the easiest to measure because frequently other areas are measuring it already. For example, the sales department is probably already measuring sales volume. Turnover is probably being measured by HR. Product quality and profitability are likely being tracked by sales and marketing, and defectives and scrap by production. We call these measurements "borrowed metrics", because you can use the measurements that already exist when you design training that supports them.

We are often asked if it is necessary to measure all of the levels for every training program. The short answer is, if you are not going to measure what you do, are you sure you should do it? There are, of course, resource limitations to keep in mind when determining how thoroughly each level should be measured. With that said, we believe that every training program should be tied to a specific behavior it should encourage, and a result it should support. Only the robustness and formality of the evaluation effort should vary.

When all four levels are measured, a compelling *Chain of Evidence*[SM] showing the value of training can be created. While we may or may not be able to prove the value of training, we can surely provide compelling evidence of its value when all four levels are measured.

For more information on the four levels and how to apply them, please refer to *Evaluating Training Programs: The Four Levels, 3rd edition,* or *Implementing the Four Levels* by Donald L. and James D. Kirkpatrick. For more information related to how the Four Levels came to be, read on for an accurate account from Don Kirkpatrick and others in the workplace learning and development field.

Chapter 2

ഇറ്റെ

Origin and History of the Kirkpatrick Four Levels

In this chapter we provide background on the origin and history of the Kirkpatrick Four Levels. We open with Don's own account and excerpts from his 1954 Ph.D. dissertation. We then offer an account from Jack Phillips, who has added onto the four levels as well as increased their visibility over the last 40 years. We also have an account from Dave Basarab, a practitioner who shares his experience with discovering, implementing, and finding the true business value of following the four levels. While the work of Jack and Dave extends beyond the Kirkpatrick Four Levels, we feel it is relevant in regards to the history and development of the model.

We provide a timeline of the key events in Don Kirkpatrick's career, and photos if they were available. Some dates are estimates, and some facts are perhaps lost forever in history. We have been as accurate as possible with the information we could unearth. We really enjoyed compiling this information; we hope you enjoy reading it!

Don Kirkpatrick's Account

I was teaching at the Management Institute at the University of Wisconsin in the 1950s. We used comment sheets at the end of each program. Most of the questions had to do with the instructor, and not much about the relevance of the program. We seldom did anything to prove that attendees had learned anything. We would ask for comments at the end of the  reaction sheet to get some indication of learning, but no attempt was made to measure it.

In 1952, I decided to go for a Ph.D. I already had an M.A. I went to the School of Education instead of the School of Business to get the degree because I thought it was time to measure learning in the programs I was teaching. My dissertation was called *Evaluating a Human Relations Program For Supervisors*. It emphasized measuring the learning in and subsequent performance from a program by the same name, which the Management Institute presented about five times a year.

My dissertation included measuring reaction, learning, and behavior, though I did not coin those terms at the time. I successfully defended my dissertation to the committee and was granted my Ph.D. in 1954.

After I got my degree, I felt I was on to something with these different aspects of measuring training effectiveness, so I decided to do some additional evaluation work for several of the companies that had sent a lot of supervisors to our program. At that point a research student assisted me in conducting patterned interviews with program attendees and their managers. We became more and more interested in measuring the change in behavior that occurred during the three months following program, and the results. It was during that post-doctoral work in the mid to late 1950's that I actually called the four aspects of evaluation *reaction, learning, behavior, results.*

I was surprised when in 1959, Bob Craig, the editor of the ASTD *Journal of the American Society of Training Directors*, asked me to write an article on the evaluation work I had done. I thought about it and told him I would write a series of four articles on the words I had chosen. You can read the original articles that were published in late 1959 and early 1960 in the following chapters of this book.

And so the ball started to roll.

I never called Reaction, Learning, Behavior, and Results the "four levels", but somebody did, and the words caught on. Trainers began to write articles about evaluation methods and processes, calling them by the level they were evaluating. The next thing I learned was that training professionals were calling my four words the "Kirkpatrick Model," a term I had never used either.

I was invited to speak to a number of organizations, and to the national conferences of ASTD, IQPC (International Quality & Productivity Center), and Training Magazine. The one comment I remember most came from a man who attended a program I taught at Ford Motor Company. He said words to the effect that I had changed the whole picture of evaluation by replacing the elusive term "evaluation" with four practical terms that were easy to understand.

Trainers in all types of organizations began to use the four words by referring to the four articles if they could find them, learning from the presentations I made, or hearing about them by word of mouth.

It wasn't until 1992 that I decided to write the book *Evaluating Training Programs: The Four Levels*. Jane Holcomb, a friend from California, suggested I do it because trainers couldn't find the articles original articles anymore, or they wanted to hear about the Four Levels from the "horse's mouth." So, the first edition of the book was published in 1994, and was followed by the second and third editions.

My son, Jim, and I then wrote the book, *Transferring Learning to Behavior* (2005), emphasizing how to be sure that Level 2

Learning would be applied on the job as Level 3 Behavior, and how to evaluate to what extent it really happened.

The third book, *Implementing The Four Levels* (2007), was designed to simplify the evaluation of the four levels by including examples, forms, and procedures from various organizations for evaluating each level.

I continue to make presentations, write, and consult on the Kirkpatrick Four Levels. Even after 50 years there is still a lot of interest. I'm happy to continue to share the message.

Excerpts From Don Kirkpatrick's Dissertation

Following are excerpts from Don's 1954 dissertation that clearly show the origin of many of the principles and techniques that are found in The Kirkpatrick Model 50 years later.

The Scope of the Study (pp. 9-11)

The primary purpose of this study at the outset was to evaluate several similar human relations training programs for industrial foremen and supervisors. During the course of the investigation, however, it seemed advisable to seek the answer to several related questions as well. Therefore, five different but related problems were included in the scope of this investigation. Chief emphasis was placed on the first of these five problems which are listed below:

1. How Effective are Human Relations Programs in Imparting Knowledge and Changing Attitudes of Industrial Foremen and Supervisors?

   The SUPERVISORY INVENTORY ON HUMAN RELATIONS was administered to the foremen before and after each program being studied. A comparison of pretest and posttest responses indicates the effectiveness of the program.

2. How Valid is the SUPERVISORY INVENTORY ON HUMAN RELATIONS As a Measure of Job Performance?

   The foremen and supervisors of the two private companies were ranked on the basis of their on-the-job performance. These ranks were related to Inventory pretest scores to determine the ability of the test to measure job performance.

3. Which Items on the Inventory Can Be Used in the Selection of Supervisors?

The responses to each of the one hundred items on the inventory were compared with the rankings of the supervisors in the two companies to determine which ones discriminate between "good" and "poor" foremen. An inventory consisting of these items can then be used as a valid device for selecting new supervisors.

4. Which Foremen Seem to Benefit Most from Human Relations Training?

The gains in Inventory scores from pretest to posttest were correlated with personal characteristics of the foremen. These characteristics included age, education, years of company experience, years of supervisory experience, number of employees supervised, and performance on the job.

5. What Subject Matter Should Be Emphasized in Future University Institutes?

A tabulation of the incorrect responses to the pretest reveals the knowledges and attitudes that foremen and supervisors bring to the University Institute. An analysis of these responses indicates the subject matter that should be stressed by Institute instructors in future programs.

The Origin of Don's Level 1: Reaction

(P. 50) Although these sheets included specific ratings for each of the instructors appearing in this program, their tabulation gives more of an indication of how much the program was enjoyed than of the knowledge gained or the attitudes changes.

(Pp. 61-62) The first indication of success of this program came from an analysis of enrollee *comment sheets* (instructor ratings) . . . In other words, the Institute was well received by those in attendance.

(P. 63)...it can be concluded that the enrollees were *highly satisfied* with the program.

(P. 70) Table X. Summary of Training *Reactions* to the Human Relations Program Conducted at the Wisconsin Paper Mill.

The Origin of Don's Level 2: Learning

(P. 50) A comparison of *pretest scores with posttest* for each foreman revealed the gain in inventory scores.

(P. 59) This investigation is concerned with how effective are Human Relations Programs in *imparting facts and principles* to industry foremen and supervisors.

The Origin of Don's Level 3: Behavior

(P. 52) How valid is the *Supervisory Inventory on Human Relations* (Don Kirkpatrick, 1953) as a measure of job performance? It was decided that the best method to answer this was to compare the Inventory with on-the-job performance.

(P. 101) There also is an urgent need to develop a well controlled technique for evaluating human relations programs by using productive criteria or other measures of job performance.

(P. 133) Exhibit K. Supervisory Merit Rating Form – Iowa Manufacturing Company

The Origin of the *Chain of Evidence*[SM] – Levels 1 through 4

(Pp. 75-76) The real purpose of the training, however, was to improve the supervisory performance of the foremen attending the sessions. The understanding, acceptance, and application of the subject matter by the supervisors, it was hoped, would raise the morale of the workers and increase the quality and quantity of production.

The Origin of "The End is the Beginning"

(P. 99) In order to make future company programs effective, the *needs of the enrollee should be determined prior to the start of the program.*

The Origin of Don's Vision for the Future

(P. 102) (final paragraph of the dissertation) It is hoped that the techniques and findings of this investigation will stimulate the determination of training needs and the objective evaluation of training results by those persons who will be concerned with human relations programs for supervisors from industry and business.

Jack Phillips' Account

Don Kirkpatrick made a significant contribution to practitioners in learning and development when he introduced the concepts of four steps for evaluation, detailing that trainers could capture reaction, learning, behavior and results. While these steps were a logical sequence of events, many trainers haven't thought about how they would evaluate learning, particularly beyond the traditional feedback and occasional testing in training programs at that time.

I was first introduced to these steps, which later became known as levels, in the 1960's while I was on the staff of the training and development function at Lockheed Aircraft (now Lockheed-Martin). We were improving our evaluation process. I was leading the effort. We captured feedback on the courses (reaction), we were doing testing (learning). We had almost no follow up to see if it made a difference. The four steps were helpful to move to the next two areas for our focus. Our particular interest was moving to results.

I worked with the levels and even used the concepts of my first ROI study, which was part of an evaluation of a cooperative education program at Lockheed. This study, which was conducted as a part of my master's thesis in statistics, showed the actual impact and monetary value of the co-op program. From that experience I became more interested in these steps. So, I contacted Don Kirkpatrick in 1974 to ask him for more details about how to accomplish these steps and the process to capture the data and perhaps any assumptions or rules to be followed, as well as guidelines and principles. At that time, Don was an extension professor at the University of Wisconsin teaching courses to managers in topics such as performance appraisal and change management (incidentally I think some of Don's best work is in those areas). In my contact, Don had indicated that he was not doing much with evaluations since he published those initial four articles that he said didn't have any more details as far as systems, processes or standards but suggested that others might be taking this further. He said he was relying on practitioners to keep working with the levels to make it successful and apply them.

With that conversation we did just that. We began to develop systematic ways to collect the data at the different levels and conduct the appropriate analysis. Our interest was in Level 4 results. However, when we examined the data we wanted to know the return on investment (ROI), which was not a part of the results Don was describing at that time. The ROI is developed by converting the results to money, and comparing them to the costs of the program. In some of our studies, we found that it was possible to have success at Level 4 with business results but actually have a negative ROI. We thought it would be proper to add an additional level because the ROI was actually a completely different level. So, that is when we added the fifth level. We also added some systematic processes and began to develop some rules for working with the data, particularly in the data analysis at Levels 4 and 5.

We published some information on our refinements in 1983 in the *Handbook of Training and Evaluation Measurement Methods*. We continued to work with this process to make it better and make it usable and to make it sustainable. This required more improvements, systematic steps, options to address specific issues, and principles and guidelines. We continued to work with the levels including ROI.

In 1992, ASTD agreed to publish a book of ROI case studies. Initially, Don had agreed to write the foreword for the book. Instead he decided to publish his own book. Since then, we have developed ten ROI casebooks and 15 books on the ROI methodology.

Over the years, I have had the pleasure of working with Don on my many programs and conferences. He is a delightful gentleman in every way. Our profession owes a lot to Don for presenting to practitioners the simple steps of evaluation. It caught on, and the levels are alive and well today.

Dave Basarab's Account

NCR Corporation, Dayton, Ohio, 1988

After 8 years of instructional design, course development, and teaching for NCR's Customer and Support Education function, I had been promoted into the role of Director of Course Development and Evaluation for the corporation. It was a newly created position with two major responsibilities: refine and hone the company's course development worldwide, and establish and implement a training evaluation system. Course development I could do; but evaluation? I had never heard of the concept, let alone implement a system. Fortunately, I had a great boss that said "That's okay, give it your best shot." So off I went.

I decided to see what existed and who was doing what with the hope of something pointing me in the right direction. I read articles, purchased books, and kept detailed notes of my findings. At that time there wasn't a lot of information available, and few corporate implementations. Most evaluation was being performed at the public school level by various college professors. Then I ran across Don's four evaluation levels and immediately knew that it was right for NCR. So I began, as I believe most people did, with Level 1 and worked forward. We standardized our Level 1 form, implemented Level 2 (pre/post-testing) in selected courses, conducted fifteen Level 3 studies, and one Level 4 ROI analysis.

I learned a lot, and during this time I called and talked to Don who gave me encouragement and suggestions for implementation. Eventually my evaluation work evolved into a corporate process for evaluations that we could institutionalize across the corporation. I thought we had some leading edge training evaluation techniques underway and published a few articles on the topic. That got some attention and soon after I was hosting benchmarking visits by other companies who wanted to know how we had implemented the four levels.

Motorola, Inc., Schaumburg, Illinois, 2001

In 2001, the premier corporate training organization in the world was Motorola University led by Bill Wiggenhorn. In response to Motorola's Six Sigma Quality Initiative, Bill formed a Quality Department that included an evaluation function. I was lucky enough to be hired to lead that team, and of course I brought Don's four levels with me. Over the next five years we implemented a standardized Level 1 system (form, quality standards, data processing, analysis, and quality review) in over a dozen locations worldwide. We created two teams using the Motorola Customer Satisfaction approach and implemented Level 2 and Level 3 processes globally. We trained hundreds of Motorola learning professionals in the corporation on not only the process, but also the skills and techniques necessary to implement the processes. We then successfully launched the processes to the enterprise.

Motorola University hosted monthly visits of learning professionals from around the world, and I had the honor of sharing our evaluation system with them. I told Don what we were doing with the 4 Levels and he asked me to write the introduction and a case study for the first edition of *Evaluating Training Programs*. I also wrote my own book, *The Training Evaluation Process*, along with numerous articles. I also made presentations at conferences such as ASTD. Finally, we began to sell our ideas to other training functions (Shell, Saturn, the Internal Revenue Service, Caterpillar) where we performed the evaluation service for them or trained them on how to do it.

V.A.L.E. Consulting, LLC, Atlanta, Georgia, 2009

A few years back I retired from corporate life and began evaluation consultation. Finding Don's work and having the opportunity to put it into practice has been one of my professional joys. I find being a consultant in the field of training evaluation challenging and enjoyable. More importantly, it's as relevant today as it was 50 years ago when Don created the Kirkpatrick Model.

Don Kirkpatrick Timeline

Education and Professional Experience

1948	**BBA**-- University of Wisconsin, Madison
1949	**MA**--University of Wisconsin, Madison
1954	**PhD**--University of Wisconsin, Madison
1949-1960	**Professor**, University of Wisconsin Management Institute, Madison
1954	**Dissertation**: *Evaluating a Human Relations Training Program for Supervisors to Measure Learning Behavior and Results*
1960-1962	**Training Manager**, International Mineral and Chemical Corporation
1962-1964	**Personnel Manager**, Bendix Products Aerospace Division
1964-1986	**Professor**, University of Wisconsin Management Institute, Milwaukee
2003-2008	**Consultant**, Kirkpatrick Consulting
2009	**Honorary Chairman**, Kirkpatrick Partners, LLC

Awards and Honors

1975	ASTD President
1982	Gordon M. Bliss Award, ASTD
1997	Elected to Training Magazine's Hall of Fame
2003	ASTD Award for Lifetime Achievement in Workplace Learning and Performance
2006	Asia HRD Congress special award for Lifetime Achievement
2006	ASTD Award: One of four "Legends" in Training and Development
2009	50th Anniversary of the Kirkpatrick Four Levels

Books and Notable Publications

1959-60   Articles on Reaction, Learning, Behavior and Results published in *Journal of the American Society of Training Directors*, ASTD

1976   Contributor to *Training and Development Handbook*, L. Craig

1978   *No Nonsense Communication, 1st edition*, K&M Publishing

1982   *How to Improve Performance Through Appraisal and Coaching*, AMACOM
1984 Best Book of the Year, ASPA (SHRM)

1985   *How to Manage Change Effectively*, Jossey-Bass
1983 Best Book of the Year, ASPA (SHRM)

1994   *Evaluating Training Programs, 1st edition,* Berrett-Koehler Publishers

1998   Compiled *Another Look at Evaluating Training Programs,* ASTD Press

Evaluating Training Programs, 2nd edition, Berrett-Koehler Publishers

2001   *Developing Supervisors and Team Leaders*, Butterworth-Heinemann

Managing Change Effectively, Butterworth-Heinemann

2005   *Transferring Learning to Behavior,* Berrett-Koehler Publishers

How to Conduct Productive Meetings, *ASTD Press*

Evaluating Training Programs, 3rd edition, Berrett-Koehler Publishers

2006   *Improving Employee Performance Through Appraisal and Coaching*, AMACOM

2007   *Implementing the Four Levels,* Berrett-Koehler Publishers

2008   Contributed to *Handbook for Workplace Learning Professionals*, ASTD Press

Don's Photo Album

Don's High School Senior Photo
1941

Tuesday, September

Madison Trio Wins Music Scholarships

Three Madison students, two of them West high school graduates, are among the 10 state pupils who have won four-year University of Wisconsin scholarships because they were "best of the best" in the university's high school music clinic last summer.

The Madison trio are Donald Kirkpatrick, 17, of 116 S. Randall ave.; Helen Samp, 18, of 2229 Eton Ridge, and Helen Holden, 17, of 2238 West Lawn ave.

Kirkpatrick, who plans to be a mechanical engineer despite his musical ability on baritone and bassoon, is the brother of Vernon Kirkpatrick, who two years ago won a similar music clinic four-year scholarship.

He will have Vernon and two more brothers in school with him this fall — Robert, a commerce senior, and Neal, a second year medical student.

Plays in Civic Symphony

Donald was graduated in June from Central high school, where he played in band and orchestra. He has been playing with the university band all summer, and plans to participate with the band and the symphony orchestra in school. He also belongs to the Madison Civic symphony. He has been playing his baritone six years and the bassoon 18 months.

Music Clinic Scholarship Article
1941

THE UNIVERSITY OF WISCONSIN
MADISON

SCHOOL OF MUSIC
OFFICE OF THE DIRECTOR
CARL BRICKEN

February 15, 1943

To whom it may concern:

Although Donald Kirkpatrick has been a member of the University of Wisconsin Band for only two years I have known him and his family for more than six years.

He has been a good student and a faithful and consistent worker. He, like his several brothers, is very honest and dependable. He has taken the initiative to do extra work which was not required of him.

He has a nice sense of humor. I have never known him to be other than a gentleman, and I am happy to write these few words recommending him as a worthy and deserving young man.

Very truly yours

Raymond F. Dvorak

Assoc. Prof. of Music
Director of Bands
University of Wisconsin

College Letter of Recommendation   1943

In the Army (Don on right)   circa 1944

In the Army (Don on right)   circa 1945

Clay Center, Kansas While in the Army (Don on left)   1944

Army Basketball Teammates (Don, second from right) 1944

Army Basketball Team Picture   1944

Don as the Madison, WI Shrine Club President, with
Governor Vernon Thompson   1955

Don Teaching a Class   circa 1955

Don (left) with Senator John. F. Kennedy   1959

Speaking   circa 1950

Donald L. Kirkpatrick has
been named supervisor
of the Milwaukee office of
the University of Wiscon-
sin — Extension Depart-
ment of Business and
Management. He will co-
ordinate the outreach and
continuing education ef-
forts of the Milwaukee
based faculty and staff
while continuing to teach
and direct programs in
management and super-
vision.

(Don on left)   circa 1950

U.W. Management Institute   1966

University News and Features

Covering the Campus

Plan Retail Seminar

Representatives of leading Madison retail stores met with staff members of the University of Wisconsin Extension Division Tuesday to map plans for a seminar for retail sales managers. Pictured, left to right, are Charles Faulhaber, of Ward-Brodt Music Co.; Morgan Manchester, Harry S. Manchester, Inc.; Dr. Donald L. Kirkpatrick, University Management Institute; and Roy Hopko, Badger Office Supplies. The retail sales seminar was tentatively scheduled for the Wisconsin Center Building early in October.

U.W. Management Institute   circa 1950

Don as ASTD President   1975

A s we begin 1975, I have mixed feelings about being your president. First of all, I am *grateful* for the confidence shown me by the National Nominating Committee and the members who elected me. Secondly, I am *humble* because of my lack of knowledge of many facets of our complex organization and the members. Thirdly, I am *enthusiastic* about the opportunity to serve the organization as the president. Finally, I am *confident* that 1975 will be an outstanding year. The potential economic and social problems are outweighed by the combination of:

- A dedicated and capable Madison staff headed by the creative, practical, and dynamic Kevin O'Sullivan.
- An able and enthusiastic Board of Directors representing all types of organizations and all geographical areas.
- Hundreds of members who serve as leaders of chapters, divisions, and special interest groups.

As the year unfolds, you will be informed of new services, new programs, and new dimensions to ASTD. All of us in leadership roles are dedicated to the proposition that 1975 will be the year when every member says:

"I sure got my money's worth from ASTD."

If I am going to be an effective president, I need assistance from two sources. First, I need guidance from God to help me make the right decisions. Also, I need the commitment and effective performance from ASTD leaders at the chapter, regional and national level.

I'd like to visit each chapter and meet each member but this is impossible. My time priorities will be given to Board meetings, national committees, Regional Conferences, ASTD Leadership Training and of course, the National Conference in Las Vegas in May. (Be sure to be in good voice because you can be sure we'll sing the ASTD Song!)

Please consider this a personal invitation to become and/or remain active in our Society in 1975. In addition, please let me know your concerns and suggestions for making ASTD more effective in improving the professional growth and performance of our members.

Sincerely,

Donald L. Kirkpatrick

ASTD President Letter   1975

Don Speaking in Saudi Arabia   circa 1975

Don With Gordon Wan   circa 1980

Don and his wife, Fern, with the Gordon M. Bliss award plaque, 1982

Don Leading the Room in "The Packer Song" at the Gordon M.
Bliss Award Acceptance   1982

Don With an Unknown Student   circa 1990

Don with *Evaluating Training Programs*   circa 1999

Chapter 3

Techniques For Evaluating Training Programs

Part 1

Unedited article originally published in the *Journal of the American Society of Training Directors*

November 1959

Techniques For Evaluating Training Programs

Because of his knowledge and experience in the field of Evaluation, we have asked Dr. Donald L. Kirkpatrick of The University of Wisconsin to write this series of four articles.

Each article will deal with one step in the Evaluation Process as Dr. Kirkpatrick sees it. Emphasis will be on techniques which training directors can use to evaluate their own programs.

DR. DONALD L. KIRKPATRICK [1]

Assistant Director
The Management Institute
The University of Wisconsin

This series of articles is based on the following assumption: That one training director cannot borrow evaluation results from another; he can, however, borrow evaluation techniques. Therefore, the techniques used by various trainers will be described without detailing the findings. Each of these four articles will discuss one of the evaluation steps, which can be summarized as follows:

Step 1 - REACTION

Step 2 - LEARNING

Step 3 - BEHAVIOR

Step 4 - RESULTS

These articles are designed to stimulate training directors to increase their efforts in evaluating training programs. It is hoped that the specific suggestions will prove helpful in these evaluation attempts.

---

[1] Also see "The Most Neglected Responsibilities of the Training Department," by Dr. Kirkpatrick in the April 1959 *Journal.*

The following quotation from Daniel M. Goodacre III[2] is most appropriate as an introduction:

"Managers, needless to say, expect their manufacturing and sales departments to yield a good return and will go to great lengths to find out whether they have done so. When it comes, to training, however, they may *expect* the return but rarely do they make a like effort to measure the actual results. Fortunately for those in charge of training programs, this philanthropic attitude, has come to be taken for granted. There is certainly no guarantee, however, that it will continue, and training directors might be well-advised to take the initiative and evaluate their programs before the day of reckoning arrives."

Step 1 - Reaction

Reaction may best be defined as how well the trainees liked a particular training program. Evaluating in terms of reaction is the same as measuring the feelings of the conferees. It is important to emphasize that it does not include a measurement of any learning that takes place. Because reaction is so easy to measure, nearly all training directors do it. However, in this writer's opinion many of these attempts do not meet the standards listed below:

GUIDES FOR EVALUATING REACTION

1. Determine what you want to find out.

2. Use a written comment sheet covering those items determined in step one above.

3. Design the form so that the reactions can be tabulated and quantified.

4. Obtain honest reactions by making the forms anonymous.

5. Allow the conferees to write in additional comments not covered by the questions that were designed to be tabulated and quantified.

The comment sheet shown in Figure 1 was used to measure reaction at the 1959 ASTD Summer Institute that was planned and coordinated by the staff of the Management Institute of the University of Wisconsin.

---

[2] "The Experimental Evaluation of Management Training: Principles and Practice," Daniel M. Goodacre III, The B. F. Goodrich Company, *Personnel,* May 1957.

Those who planned this ASTD Program were interested in reactions to: Subject, technique (lecture vs. discussion), and the performance of the conference leader. Therefore, the form was designed accordingly. So the reactions could be readily tabulated and quantified, the conferees were asked to place a check in the appropriate spaces.

In question 3 concerning the leader, it was felt that a more meaningful rating would be given the leader if the conferees considered items A through G before checking the "overall rating." This question was designed to prevent a conference leader's personality from dominating group reaction.

Question 4 allowed the conferees to suggest any improvements that came to mind. The optional signature was used so that follow-up discussions with conferees could be done. In the 1959 Summer ASTD Institute, about half of the conferees signed their names. With this type of group, the optional signature did not affect the honesty of their answers, in all probability. It is strongly suggested that unsigned sheets be used in most meetings, however.

This ASTD reaction sheet was used at the conclusion of every session in the institute program. Therefore, the conferees rated each conference leader for his contribution to the program. In many internal training programs, a series of meetings will be held and the reaction sheet will not be used until the end of the last session. This is especially true when one conference leader conducts the entire program. In this case, a comment sheet like the ASTD one might be adapted to the situation and modifications made.

In doing research on the subject of evaluation, this writer received a very practical suggestion from Richard Johnson, past president of the New York chapter of ASTD. Mr. Johnson suggested that the comment sheets be given to the enrollees before the program is over so that the suggestions can be used in improving the last section of the training program. For example, where a training program consists of a series of nine sessions, the comment sheet should be given to conferees at the end of the third session. Their comments and suggestions should be taken into consideration to make the last six sessions more effective.

ASTD Institute

Leader_____

Subject_____

Date   _____

1. Was the subject pertinent to your needs and interests?

   ☐ No   ☐ To Some Extent   ☐ Very Much So

2. How was the ratio of lecture to discussion?

   ☐ Too Much Lecture ☐ OK   ☐ Too Much Discussion

3. How about the Leader?

                                        Excellent Very Good Fair Poor
                                                  Good

A. How well did he state objectives?

B. How well did he keep the session alive and
interesting?

C. How well did he use the blackboard, charts
and other aids?

D. How well did he summarize during the session?

E. How well did he maintain a friendly and helpful
manner?

F. How well did he illustrate and clarify the
points?

G. How was his summary at the close of the
session?

What is your overall rating of the leader?

   ☐ Excellent   ☐ Very Good   ☐ Good   ☐ Fair   ☐ Poor

What would have made the session more effective?

_____

_____

_____

_____

Signature (optional)_____

Figure 1   RATING CHART

How to Supplement the Evaluation of the Conferees

So far in this article, the techniques for measuring the reactions of the enrollees have been discussed. It has been emphasized that the form should be designed so that tabulations can be readily made. In this writer's opinion, too many comment sheets are still being used in which the conferees are asked to write in their answers to questions. Using a form of this kind, it becomes very difficult to summarize comments and to determine patterns of reaction.

At The Management Institute of The University of Wisconsin, every session is evaluated in terms of the reactions of the conferees. This has been done for more than 10 years. Many times, the coordinator of the program felt that the group reaction was not a fair evaluation of the effectiveness of the program.

Sometimes the staff men felt that the conference leader's personality made such an impression on the group that he received a very high rating. In other sessions, the coordinator felt that the conference leader received a low rating because he did not have a dynamic personality. Frequently, in the opinion of the coordinator, the latter type of conference leader presented much more practical and helpful material than the former. Therefore, The Management Institute adopted a procedure by which every conference leader is rated by the coordinator as well as by the group. The form in Figure 2 is used for the coordinator's evaluation.

This procedure in which the coordinator of the program also evaluates each conference leader was used in the 1959 ASTD Summer Institute. It was found that a coordinator's rating was usually close to the group's rating, but in some instances it varied considerably. A combination of the two ratings was used by the Management Institute staff in evaluating the effectiveness of each conference leader. In selecting and orienting future conference leaders for ASTD Institutes, both of the evaluations will be taken into consideration.

It is suggested that the training director in each company consider this approach. A trained observer such as the Training Director or another qualified person would fill out an evaluation form independent of the group's reactions. A comparison of the two would give the best indication of the effectiveness of the program.

STAFF RATING OF LEADER

Rating   Name of Leader   Subject   Date   Rater's Initial

Very Much So   To Some Extent   No

A. PREPARATION

1. Did he prepare for the meeting?

2. Was his preparation geared to the group?

B. CONDUCTING

1. Did he read his material?

2. Did he hold the interest of the group?

3. Was he enthusiastic – dynamic?

4. Did he use visual aids?
    If yes, what aids?

5. Did he present his material clearly?

6. Did he help the group apply the material?

7. Did he adequately cover the subject?

8. Did he summarize during conference and at end?

9. Did he involve the group?
    If yes, how?

C. CONSTRUCTIVE COMMENTS

1. What would you suggest to improve future sessions?

_____

D. POTENTIAL

1. With proper coaching, what would be the highest rating he could achieve? _____

E. ADDITIONAL COMMENTS

_____

_____

_____

Figure 2   LEADER RATING SHEET

RESULTS OF UNIVERSITY OF WISCONSIN MANAGEMENT INSTITUTE PROGRAM QUESTIONNAIRE

Key	*Programs*
A	Modern Leadership for Middle Management
B	Supervisors' Leadership in Cost Control
C	Developing Supervisory Skills
D	Human Relations for Foremen & Supervisors
E	Leadership and Growth
F	Creative Thinking for Supervisors
G	Human Relations for New Foremen
T	Totals

	A	B	C	D	E	F	G	T
Questionnaires returned:	3	3	5	11	5	1	1	29

1. I thought the program was:

	A	B	C	D	E	F	G	T
A. Very well organized and helpful	3	3	5	11	5	1	1	29
B. It was of some value								
C. It was poorly organized and a waste of time								

2. In reference to the subject content:

	A	B	C	D	E	F	G	T
A. It was all theory and of little practical value								
B. It was both theory and practical	3	2	2	3	1	1		11
C. It was very practical and useful	0	1	3	9	4	1	1	19

3. Concerning the quality of the instruction:

	A	B	C	D	E	F	G	T
A. The instruction was excellent	2	3	4	11	4	1	1	26
B. I would consider the instruction average	1		1					2
C. The instruction was of poor quality								

Figure 3   OSCAR MAYER & CO. EVALUATION FORM

Measuring Reactions To Outside Training Programs

The forms and suggestions that have been described above will apply best to an internal training program. Since many companies send their management people to outside training programs at universities, American Management Association, National Industrial Conference Board, etc., it is suggested that the reaction of each person attending such a program be measured. Lowell Reed, Training Director of the Oscar Mayer & Company of Madison, Wisconsin, uses the form in Figure 3 for evaluating the reaction to the University of Wisconsin -Management Institute program.

In this situation, Oscar Mayer & Company is not interested in the reaction to specific leaders. They are interested in reaction to the over-all program to determine whether or not to send other foremen and supervisors. In other words, this particular questionnaire was designed to fit the need of the Oscar Mayer & Company. In addition to the tabulated responses described above, an opportunity was given each person to write in additional comments.

Another company uses the form in Figure 4 to evaluate the reaction of their managers who attend an outside program:

REACTION TO SUPERVISORY INSTITUTES BY FOREMEN
AND SUPERVISORS WHO HAVE PARTICIPATED

IN GENERAL

1. How worthwhile was the Institute(s) for you?

☐ Very worthwhile

☐ Fairly worthwhile

☐ Not very worthwhile

☐ A waste of time

2. Did the Institute have:

☐ Too much theory and not enough of the practical

☐ Too much of the practical and not enough theory

☐ About the right combination of theory and practice

HOW THE INSTITUTE WAS CONDUCTED

3. On the whole, the course was conducted

☐ Very well

☐ Fairly well

☐ Poorly

☐ Very poorly

4. Lecture and discussion

   ☐ Too much lecture

   ☐ Too much discussion

   ☐ About the right amount of each

5. Discussion leaders

   ☐ Too many from the University

   ☐ Too many from business and industry

   ☐ O.K.

6. Visual aids

   ☐ Not enough movies, charts, etc.

   ☐ Too much use of demonstrations, blackboards, movies, charts, etc.

   ☐ O.K.

APPLICATION OF THE COURSE

7. Did the Institute apply to your particular operations?

   ☐ Yes ☐ Partly ☐ No

FOLLOW-UP

8. Would you like to attend another institute?

   ☐ Yes ☐ No

   Comment

9. Should these Institutes run for ☐ 5 days ☐ 4 days ☐ 3 days.

10. Please list 3 of your main problems:

   1. _____

      _____

   2. _____

      _____

   3. _____

      _____

11. Comments or suggestions

Figure 4 SUPERVISOR INSTITUTE PROGRAM EVALUATION
FORM

Summary and Conclusion

The first step in the evaluation process is to measure the reactions to training programs. It is important to determine how people feel about the programs they attend. Decisions by top management are frequently made on the basis of one or two comments they receive from people who have attended. A supervisory training program may be cancelled because one superintendent told the plant manager that "this program is for the birds."

Also, people must like a training program to obtain maximum benefit from it. According to Spencer, for example, "for maximum learning you must have interest and enthusiasm." In a talk given by Cloyd Steinmetz, past president of ASTD, "It is not enough to say, 'boys, here is the information, take it!' We must make it interesting and motivate them to want to take it."

To evaluate effectively, training directors should begin by doing a good job of measuring reactions and feelings of people who participate. It is important to do so in an organized fashion using written comment sheets, which have been designed to obtain the desired reactions. It is also strongly suggested that the form be so designed that the comments can be tabulated and quantified. In the experience of the staff of The Management Institute, it is also desirable to have the coordinator, training director, or another trained observer make his own appraisal of the session in order to supplement the reactions of enrollees. The combination of these two evaluations is more meaningful than either one by itself.

Companies who send their people to attend outside institutes and conferences should make an effort to evaluate the reactions to these programs. Several suggested forms have been described.

When a training director has effectively measured the *reactions* of conferees and finds them to be very favorable, he can feel very proud. However, he should also feel humble because his evaluation measurement has only begun. Even though he has done a masterful job of measuring the reaction of the group, he still has no assurance that any learning has taken place. Neither has he any indication that the behavior of the participants will change because of the training program. And still farther away is any indication of the results that can be attributed to the training program. These 3 steps in the evaluation process-learning, behavior, and results will be discussed in detail in the next three articles of this series on Evaluation.

Chapter 4

ഇൗൟൟ

Techniques For Evaluating Training Programs

Part 2

Unedited article originally published in the *Journal of the American Society of Training Directors*

December 1959

December 1959

The Second in a Series of Four Articles . . .

Techniques For Evaluating Training Programs
Part 2 – Learning

DR. DONALD KIRKPATRICK*

We have emphasized in the first article (November, 1959 Journal, pg. 3) that the reaction of the conferees is important in evaluating the training program. From an analysis of reactions, a training director can determine how well the program was accepted. He can also obtain comments and suggestions, which will be helpful in improving future programs. It is important to obtain favorable reaction because:

1. Decisions on future training activities are frequently based on the reactions of one or more key persons.

2. The more favorable the reaction to the program, the more likely the conferees are to pay attention and learn the principles, facts, and techniques that are discussed.

However, it is important to recognize that favorable reaction to a program *does not assure* learning. All of us have attended meetings in which the conference leader or speaker used enthusiasm, showmanship, visual aids, and illustrations to make his presentation well accepted by the group. A careful analysis of the subject content would reveal that he said practically nothing of value – but he did it very well. At our Management Institute of the University of Wisconsin, for example, this has been true on a number of cases. (Less and less, I hasten to add).

---

* Dr. Kirkpatrick has recently left his former position as Assistant Director, The Management Institute, The University of Wisconsin to accept a new assignment with International Minerals and Chemical Corp., Skokie, IL.

Therefore, it is important to determine objectively the amount of learning that takes place. This article is aimed at suggesting ways and means for measuring this learning.

Learning Defined

There are several definitions for learning. For the purpose of this article, learning is defined in a rather limited way as follows: What principles, facts, and techniques were understood and absorbed by the conference? In other words, we are not concerned with the on-the-job use of these principles, facts and techniques. This application will be discussed in the third article dealing with "Behavior."

Guideposts for Evaluating in Terms of Learning

Several guideposts should be used in establishing a procedure for measuring the amount of learning that takes place.

1. The learning of *each conferee* should be measured so that quantitative results can be determined.

2. A before-and-after approach should be used so that any learning can be related to the program.

3. As far as possible, the learning should be measured on an *objective* basis.

4. Where possible, a control group (not receiving the training) should be used to compare with the experimental group, which receives the training.

5. Where possible, the evaluation results should be analyzed statistically so that learning can be proven in terms of correlation or level of confidence.

These guideposts indicate that evaluation in terms of learning is much more difficult than evaluation in terms of reaction as described in the first article. A knowledge of statistics, for example, is necessary. In many cases, the training department will have to call on the assistance of a statistician to plan the evaluation procedures, analyze the data, and interpret the results.

Suggested Methods

CLASSROOM PERFORMANCE

It is relatively easy to measure the learning that takes place in training programs that are teaching skills. The following programs would fall under this category: Job Instruction Training; Work Simplification; Interviewing

Skills; Induction Techniques; Reading Improvement; Effective Speaking; and Effective Writing. Classroom activities such as demonstrations, individual performance of the skill being taught, and discussions following a role playing situation can be used as evaluation techniques. The training director can organize these in such a way that he will obtain a fairly objective evaluation of the learning that is taking place.

For example, in a course that is teaching Job Instruction Training to foremen, each foreman will demonstrate in front of the class the skills of JIT. From his performance, the training director can tell whether or not he has learned the principles of JIT and can use them, at least in a classroom situation. In a Work Simplification program, each conferee can be required to fill out a "flow-process chart" and the training director can determine whether or not he knows how to do it. In a Reading Improvement program, the reading speed and comprehension of each participant can be readily determined by his classroom performance. In an Effective Speaking program, each conferee is normally required to give a number of talks and an alert training director can measure to some extent the amount of learning that is taking place by observing his successive performances.

So in these kinds of situations, an evaluation of the learning can be built into the program. If it is organized and implemented properly, the training director can obtain a fairly objective measure of the amount of learning that has taken place. He can set up before-and-after situations in which each conferee demonstrates whether or not he knows the principles and techniques being taught.

In every program therefore, where skills of some kind are being taught, the training director should plan systematic classroom evaluation to measure the learning.

PAPER-AND-PENCIL TESTS

Where principles and facts are taught rather than techniques, it is more difficult to evaluate learning. The most common technique is the paper-and-pencil test. In some cases, standardized tests can be purchased to measure learning. In other cases, the training director must construct his own.

To measure the learning in human relations programs, two standardized tests are quite widely used in business and industry. The first is "HOW SUPERVISE?" by File and Remmers. This is published by The

Psychological Corporation of New York and has been used by a number of companies on a before-and-after basis to measure the learning that takes place. A newer test is the "SUPERVISORY INVENTORY ON HUMAN RELATIONS" by Kirkpatrick and Planty.[1] Following are sample test items from the latter (answered by circling "A" for agree or "DA" for disagree):

PLEASE ANSWER ALL STATEMENTS EVEN IF YOU ARE NOT SURE

Copyright 1956 by D. L. Kirkpatrick

Published by Dr. Earl Planty and Dr. Donald Kirkpatrick, 506 Toepfer Avenue, Madison, Wis.

1. Anyone is able to do almost any job if he tries hard enough. A DA
2. Intelligence consists of what we've learned since we were born. A DA
3. If a supervisor knows all about the work to be done, he is therefore qualified to teach others how to do it. A DA
4. We are born with certain attitudes and there is little we can do to change them. A DA
5. A supervisor should not praise members of his department when they do a good job because they will ask for a raise. A DA
6. A well-trained working force is a result of maintaining a large training department. A DA
7. A supervisor would lose respect if he asked employees to help him solve problems that concern them. A DA
8. In making a decision, a good supervisor is concerned with his employees' feelings about the decision. A DA
9. The supervisor is closer to his employees than he is to management. A DA
10. The best way to train a new employee is to have him watch a good employee at the job. A DA
11. Before deciding on the solution to a problem, a list of possible solutions should be made and compared. A DA
12. A supervisor should be willing to listen to almost anything the employees want to tell him. A DA

---

[1] Complimentary copy available from Dr. Donald Kirkpatrick, 541 Woodside Terrace, Madison, WI

There are also standardized tests available in such areas as Creativity and Economics. In following the guideposts that were suggested in the beginning of this article, this kind of a standardized test should be used in the following manner:

1. The tests should be given to all conferees prior to the program.

2. If possible, it should also be given to a control group, which is to the experimental group.

3. These pretests should be analyzed in terms of two approaches: In the first place, the total score of each person should be tabulated. Secondly, the responses to each item of the inventory should be tabulated in terms of right and wrong answers. This second tabulation not only enables a training man to evaluate the program but also gives him some tips on the knowledge and understanding of the group prior to the program. This means that in the classroom, he can stress those items most frequently misunderstood.

4. After the program is over, the same test or its equivalent should be given to the conferees and also to the control group. A comparison of pretest and posttest scores and responses to individual items can then be made. A statistical analysis of this data will reveal the effectiveness of the program in terms of learning.

One important word of caution must be made. Unless the test or inventory accurately covers the material presented, it will not be a valid measure of the effectiveness of the learning. Frequently a standardized test will cover only part of the material presented in the course. Therefore, only that part of the course covered in the inventory is being evaluated. Likewise, if certain items on the inventory are *not* being covered, no change in these items can be expected.

There are also many examples where training directors and others responsible for programs have developed their own paper-and-pencil tests to measure learning in their programs. For example, the American Telephone and Telegraph Company has incorporated into their "Personal Factors in Management" program, a short test measuring the sensitivity and empathy. First, each individual is asked to rank in order of importance, 10 items dealing with human relations. They are then assigned to a group, which is asked to work 15 minutes at the task of arriving at a group ranking of the 10 statements. Following this 15 minute "heated discussion," each individual is asked to complete a short inventory, which includes the following questions:

1. A. Were you satisfied with the performance of the group?
☐ Yes   ☐ No

   B. How many will say that they were satisfied with the performance of the group? _____

2. A. Do you feel that two or three members dominated the discussion?
☐ Yes   ☐ No

   B. How many will say that they thought the discussion was dominated by two or three members? _____

3. A. Did you have any feelings about the items being ranked that, for some reason, you felt it wise not to express during the discussion?

   ☐ Yes   ☐ No

   B. How many will say that they had such feelings? _____

4. A. Did you talk as often as you wished to in the discussion?
☐ Yes   ☐ No

   B. How many will say that they talked as often as they wished to? ____

The successive class sessions then attempt to teach each conferee to be more sensitive to the feelings and ideas of other people. Later in the course, another "empathy" test is given to see whether there is an increase in sensitivity.

At the ASTD Summer Institute in Madison, Wisconsin in 1959, Dr. Earl Planty of the University of Illinois introduced a test on decision-making.[2] Several items from that test follow:

1. If my boss handed back to me a well done piece of work and asked me to make changes on it, I would
   ☐ prove to him that the job is better without changes.
   ☐ do what he says and point out where he is wrong.
   ☐ complete the changes without comment.
   ☐ request a transfer from his department.

---

[2] Published by Martin M. Bruce, 71 Hansen Lane, Rochelle, New York.

2. If I were office manager and one of the best clerks kept complaining about working conditions, I would

☐ try to determine the basis for the complaints.

☐ transfer him to some other section.

☐ point out to him that his complaining is bad for morale.

☐ ask him to write out his complaints for your superior.

3. If my supervisor criticized my work, I would

☐ compare my record with co-workers for him.

☐ explain the reason for poor performance to him.

☐ ask him why he selected me for criticism.

☐ ask him for suggestions about how to improve.

4. If I were setting up a new procedure in an office, I would

☐ do it on my own without enlisting anyone's aid.

☐ ask my superiors for suggestions.

☐ ask the people who work under me for suggestions.

☐ discuss it with my friends who are outside of the company.

This test or one like it can be given before and after a program on decision making to determine whether or not the participants learned the principles and procedures taught in the course.

In Morris A. Savitt's article called "Is Management Training Worthwhile?"[3] he described a program he evaluated. He devised a questionnaire, which was given at the beginning of the program "to determine how much knowledge of management principles and practices the conferees had at the beginning." At the end of the ten-week program, the same questionnaire was administered to test the progress made during the course. This is an example of a questionnaire tailored to a specific program.

Daniel M. Goodacre III of the B. F. Goodrich Company has done a great deal of work in this area. He has developed and used achievement tests which are given before and after training programs to determine the amount of learning.

---

[3] Personnel, September-October, 1957, American Management Association.

And so we see that the paper-and pencil test can be used effectively in measuring the learning that takes place in a training program. It should be emphasized again that the approach to this kind of evaluation should be systematic and statistically oriented. A comparison of before and after scores and responses can then be made to prove how much learning has taken place.

Nile Soik of the Allen-Bradley Company described an additional evaluation procedure in his article in the March 1958 issue of the *Journal of the ASTD*. Not only did he use the SUPERVISORY INVENTORY ON HUMAN RELATIONS before and after the program, but he also administered it six months later. He was measuring the forgetting that took place in the period following the program.

Summary

It is easy to see, then, that it is much more difficult to measure *learning* than it is to measure *reaction* to a program. A great deal of work is required in planning the evaluation procedure, in analyzing the data that is obtained, and interpreting the results. Wherever possible, it is suggested that training directors devise their own methods and techniques. As has been pointed out in this article, it is relatively easy to plan classroom demonstrations and presentations to measure learning where the program is aimed at the teaching of skills. Where principles and facts are the objectives of the training program, it is advisable to use a paper-and-pencil test. Where suitable standardized tests can be found, it is easier to use them. In many programs, however, it is not possible to find a standardized test and the training man must use his skill and ingenuity in devising his own measuring instrument.

If a training director can prove that his program has been effective in terms of learning as well as in terms of reaction, he has objective data to use in selling future programs and in increasing his status and position in the company.

Chapter 5

ഊഗ്ഋഋഒഋ

Techniques For Evaluating Training Programs

Part 3

Unedited article originally published in the *Journal of the American Society of Training Directors*

January 1960

The Third in a Series of Four Articles . . .

Techniques For Evaluating
Training Programs
Part 3 – Behavior

DR. DONALD L. KIRKPATRICK
Advanced Management Development Administrator
International Minerals and Chemical Corporation
Skokie, Illinois

In the two previous articles in this series, we talked about techniques for evaluating "training programs in terms of (1) REACTION and (2) LEARNING. It was emphasized that in our evaluations, we can borrow techniques but we cannot borrow results.

A personal experience may be the best way of starting this third article dealing with changes in behavior. When I joined The Management Institute of The University of Wisconsin in 1949, one of my first assignments was to sit through a one-week course on "Human Relations for Foremen and Supervisors." During the week I was particularly impressed by a foreman named Herman from a Milwaukee company. Whenever a conference leader asked a question requiring a good understanding of human relations principles and techniques, Herman was the first one who raised his hand. He had all the answers in terms of good human relations approaches. I was very much impressed and I said to myself "if I were in this industry, I would like to work for a man like Herman."

It so happened that I had a first cousin who was working for that company. And oddly enough, Herman was his boss. At my first opportunity, I talked with my cousin, Jim, and asked him about Herman. Jim told me that Herman may know all the principles and techniques of human relations, but he certainly does not practice them on the job. He performed as the typical "bull-of-the-woods" who had little consideration for the feelings and ideas of his subordinates.

At this time I began to realize there may be a big difference between knowing principles and techniques and using them on the job.

Robert Katz, Professor at Dartmouth wrote an article in the July-August 1956 issue of the *Harvard Business Review.* The article was called "Human Relations Skills Can Be Sharpened." And he said: "If a person is going to change his job behavior, five basic requirements must exist":

1. He must want to improve.

2. He must recognize his own weaknesses.

3. He must work in a permissive climate.

4. He must have some help from someone who is interested and skilled.

5. He must have an opportunity to try out the new ideas.

It seems that Katz has put his finger on the problems that exist in a transition between learning and changes in behavior on the job.

Evaluation of training programs in terms of on· the job behavior is more difficult than the reaction and learning evaluations described in the two previous articles. A more scientific approach is needed and many factors must be considered. During the last few years a number of attempts have been made and more and more effort is being put in this direction.

Several guideposts are to be followed in evaluating training programs in terms of behavioral changes:

1.   A *systematic* appraisal should be made of on-the-job performance on a *before-and-after* basis.

2.   The appraisal of performance should be made by one or more of the following groups (The more the better):

   A. The person receiving the training

   B. His superior or superiors

   C. His subordinates

   D. His peers or other people thoroughly familiar with his performance.

3.   A statistical analysis should be made to compare before and after performance and relate changes to the training program.

4:   The post-training appraisal should be made three months or more after the training so that the trainees have an opportunity to put into practice what they have learned. Subsequent appraisals may add to the validity of the study.

5.   A control group (not receiving the training) should be used.

Some of the best evaluation studies are briefly described below.

The Fleishman-Harris Studies[1]

To evaluate a training program that had been conducted at the Central School of The International Harvester Company, Fleishman developed a study design and a battery of research instruments for measuring the effectiveness of the training. Seven paper-and-pencil questionnaires were used and the trainees, their superiors, and their subordinates were all surveyed.

To supplement the data that Fleishman had discovered, Harris conducted a follow-up study in the same organization. He used a before-and-after measure of job performance and worked with experimental and control groups. He obtained information from the trainees themselves as well as from their subordinates.

Survey Research Center Studies[2]

The Survey Research Center of the University of Michigan has contributed much to evaluation of training programs in terms of on-the-job behavior. To measure the effectiveness of a human relations program conducted by Dr. Norman Maier at the Detroit Edison Co., and to measure the results of an experimental program called "feedback," a scientific approach to evaluation was used. A basic design was to use a before-and-after measure of on-the-job performance with experimental as well as control groups. The supervisors receiving the training as well as their subordinates were surveyed in order to compare the results of the research.

---

[1] Fleishman, E. A., Harris, E. F., Buntt, H. E., "Leadership and Supervision in Industry." Personnel Research Board, Ohio State University, Columbus, Ohio, 1955, page "llO

[2] Mann, Dr. Floyd, "Human Relations in the Industrial Setting." Survey Research Center, University of Michigan, Ann Arbor, Michigan.

The instrument used for measuring these changes was an attitude and opinion survey designed and developed by the Survey Research Center.

The Lindholm Study[3]

This study was carried out in the home office of a small insurance company during the period of October 1950 to May 1951. A questionnaire developed as part of the research program of the Industrial Relations Center of the University of Minnesota was used. It was given on a before-and-after basis to the subordinates of those who took the training. No control group was used. A statistical analysis of the before-and-after results of the attitude survey determined the effectiveness of the program in terms of on-the-job behavior.

The Blocker Study[4]

A different approach was used in the study conducted in an insurance company having approximately 600 employees. Fifteen supervisors who took a course on "Democratic Leadership" were analyzed during the three-month period following the course. Eight of the supervisors were classified as democratic and seven were classified as authoritarian based on their behavior prior to the program.

During the three-month period immediately following the program, the changes in behavior of the supervisors were analyzed through a study of their interview records. They used standard printed forms, which made provision for recording the reason for the interview, attitude of the employee, comments of the supervisor, and action taken, if any. Each supervisor was required to make a complete record of each interview. They did not know that these records were to be used for an evaluation study. There were a total of 376 interviews with 186 employees.

The interview records were classified as authoritarian or democratic. The changes in interview approach and techniques were studied during the three-month period following the course to determine if on-the-job behavior of the supervisors changed.

---

[3] Lindholm, T. R., "Supervisory Training and Employee Attitudes," *Journal of the ASTD* Nov.-Dec. 1953

[4] Blocker, C. E., "Evaluation of a Human Relations Training Course," *Journal of the ASTD* May-June 1955

The Tarnopol Approach[5]

In his article called "Evaluate Your Training Program," Tarnopol suggests the approach to use as well as a specific example of an evaluation experiment. He believes in the employee attitude survey given on a before-and-after basis using control as well as experimental groups. He stresses "in our experience, five employees is a good minimum for measuring the behavior of their supervisor." He also stresses "although canned questionnaires are available, it is advisable to use measuring instruments that are specifically suited to the requirements of both your company and your training program."

In his employee attitude approach, Tarnopol has suggested inserting some neutral questions, which do not relate to the training being given. This is an added factor in interpreting the results of the research.

The Moon-Hariton Study[6]

Their study was made in an Engineering Section of a department of the General Electric Company in 1956. A representative of the Psychological Corporation assisted the staff of the General Electric Company was assisted by a representative of the Psychological Corporation.

In the spring of 1958, two years after the adoption of a new appraisal and training program, a decision was made to attempt to evaluate its effectiveness. It was felt that the opinion of the subordinates about changes in the managers' attitudes and behavior would provide a better measure than what the managers themselves thought about the benefits of the program. Thus a questionnaire was designed to obtain the subordinates' views about changes in their managers. Nevertheless, it was felt that the opinions of the manager would add to the picture. Accordingly, they were also surveyed.

The questionnaire asked the respondents to compare present conditions with what they were two years ago. In other words, instead of measuring the attitudes before and after the program, the subordinates and the managers were asked to indicate what changes had taken place during the last two years.

---

[5] Tarnopol, Lester, "Evaluate Your Training Program," *Journal of the ASTD,* Mar.-Apr.1957

[6] Moon, C. G., Hadton, Theodore, "Evaluating an Appraisal and Feedback Training Program," *Personnel,* Nov.-Dec. 1958

The Buchanan-Brunstetter Study[7]

At the Republic Aviation Corporation, an attempt was made to measure the results of a training program. The questionnaire was used and an experimental and a control group were measured. The experimental group had received the training program during the past year while the control group was going to receive it during the following year. The subordinates of the supervisors in each one of these groups were asked to complete a questionnaire, which related to the on-the-job behavior of their supervisor. After answering the questionnaire in which they described the job behavior of their supervisor, they were asked to go over the questionnaire again and to place a check opposite any items: "(1) which you think are *more* effectively done now than a year ago; (2) which you think are *less* effectively done now than a year ago."

In this experiment as well as in the Moon-Hariton approach, the subordinates were asked to indicate what changes in behavior had taken place during the last year. This was done because a before measure of their behavior had not been made.

The Stroud Study[8]

A new training program called "Personal Factors in Management" was evaluated at the Bell Telephone Company of Pennsylvania by Peggy Stroud. Several different approaches were used to compare the results and obtain a more valid indication of on-the-job behavioral changes that resulted from the program.   The first step was the formulation of a questionnaire to be filled out by four separate groups: (1) conferees (2) controlees (supervisors not taking the course) (3) superiors of the conferees (4) superiors of the controllees.

The first part of the questionnaire was the "Consideration Scale" taken from the leader behavior description questionnaire originated in the Ohio State leadership studies. The second part of the questionnaire was called the Critical Incident section in which the conferee and control groups were asked to describe four types of incidents that had occurred on the job. The

---

[7] Buchanan, P. C., Brunstetter, P. H., "A Research Approach to Management Improvement," *Journal of the ASTD,* Jan. and Feb., 1959.

[8] Stroud, P. V., "Evaluating a Human Relations Training Program," *Personnel,* Nov.-Dec.1959.

third and final section of the questionnaire applied to the conferees only. They were asked to rate the extent to which they felt the training course had helped them achieve each of its five stated objectives.

It was decided to conduct an extensive evaluation of the training program after the program had begun. Therefore it was not possible to make a before and after comparison. In this study, an attempt was made to get the questionnaire respondents to compare on-the-job behavior before the program with that following the program. According to Miss Stroud, it would have been better to measure behavior prior to the program and then compare it to behavior measured after the program.

This study called "Evaluating A Human Relations Training Program" is one of the best attempts this writer has discovered. The various evaluation results are compared and fairly concrete interpretations made.

The Sorensen Study[9]

The most comprehensive research that has been done to evaluate the effectiveness of a training program in terms of on-the-job behavior was made at the Crotonville Advanced Management Course of the General Electric Company. It was called the "Observed Changes Enquiry."

The purpose of the "enquiry" was to answer these questions:

1. Have manager graduates of General Electric's Advanced Management Courses of 1956 been observed to have changed in their manner of managing?

2. What inferences may be made from similarities and differences of changes observed in graduates and non-graduates?

First of all, the managers (graduates and non-graduates alike) were asked to indicate changes they had observed in their own manner of managing during the previous twelve months. Secondly, subordinates were asked to describe changes they had observed in the managers during the past twelve months. Thirdly, their peers (looking sideways) were asked to describe changes in behavior. And finally, the superiors of the control and experimental groups were asked to describe the same changes in behavior.

---

[9] Sorensen, Olav, "The Observed Changes Enquiry," Manager Development Consulting Service, General Electric Company, Crotonville, New York, May 15, 1958

This gave Sorensen an excellent opportunity to compare the observed changes of all four groups.

In this extensive research, Sorensen used experimental as well as control groups. He also used four different approaches to measure observed changes. These include the man himself, his subordinates, his peers, and his superiors. In this research, he did not use a before-and-after measure but rather asked each of the participants to indicate what changes, if any, had taken place during the past year.

Summary and Conclusions

The purpose of this article has been to describe briefly some of the best experiments that have been used to measure effectiveness of training programs in terms of on-the-job behavior. Only the methods and instruments used in these studies have been mentioned. The results, although interesting, cannot be borrowed by other training directors but the techniques can.

For those interested in evaluating in terms of behavioral changes, it is strongly suggested that these studies be carefully analyzed. The references following this article indicate where the detailed articles can be found.

Once more I would like to emphasize that the future of training directors and their programs depends to a large extent on their effectiveness. To determine effectiveness, attempts must be made to measure in scientific and statistical terms. This article, dealing with changes in behavior resulting from training programs, indicates a very complicated procedure. But it is worthwhile and necessary if training programs are going to increase in effectiveness and their benefits made clear to top management.

It is obvious that very few training directors have the background, skill and time to engage in extensive evaluations. It is therefore frequently necessary to call on statisticians, research people, and consultants for advice and help.

Chapter 6

ഇഗ്ഗ്ഗ്ഗ

Techniques For Evaluating Training Programs

Part 4

Unedited article originally published in the *Journal of the American Society of Training Directors*

February 1960

February 1960

The Final in a *Series* of *Four Articles* . . .

Techniques For Evaluating Training Programs
Part 4 – Results[1]

DR. DONALD L. KIRKPATRICK
Advanced Management Development Administrator
International Minerals and Chemical Corporation
Skokie, Illinois

The objectives of most training programs can be stated in terms of results desired. These results could be classified as: reduction of costs; reduction of turnover and absenteeism; reduction of grievances; increase in quality and quantity of production; or improved morale which, it is hoped, will lead to some of the previously stated results. From an evaluation standpoint, it would be best to evaluate training programs directly in terms of results desired. There are, however, so many complicating factors that it is extremely difficult if not impossible to evaluate certain kinds of programs in terms of results. Therefore, it is recommended that training directors begin to evaluate in terms of the three criteria described in the preceding articles.[1] First of all, determine the *reactions of* the trainees. Secondly, attempt to measure what *learning* takes place. And thirdly, try to measure the changes in on-the-job behavior. As has been stressed in the previous articles, these criteria are listed in increasing order of difficulty.

As I survey literature on evaluation, I find more and more articles being written on this subject. Nearly every issue of the Journal of the ASTD contains one or more articles. It is interesting to note that few of them deal with evaluation in terms of results. And this is because it is usually a difficult evaluation to make.

---

1. See November, December, 1959 and January 1960 *Journal of the ASTD.*

Certain kinds of training programs though, are relatively easy to evaluate in terms of results. For example, in teaching clerical personnel to do a more effective typing job, you can measure the number of words per minute on a before and after basis. If you are trying to reduce grievances in your plant, you can measure the number of grievances before and after the training program. If you are attempting to reduce accidents, a before and after measure can be made. One word of caution, however. E. C. Keachie stated it as follows in an issue of the *Journal of the ASTD:* "Difficulties in the evaluation of training are evident at the outset in the problem technically called 'the separation of variables'; that is, how much of the improvement is due to training as compared to other factors?" This is the problem that makes it very difficult to measure results that can be attributed directly to a specific training program.

Below are described several evaluations that have been made in terms of results. They do not offer specific formulas for other training directors to follow, but they do suggest procedures and approaches which can be effectively used.

Safety Programs

Many attempts have been made to evaluate the effectiveness of safety training programs in terms of lost-time accidents. One study was' conducted by Philip E. Beekman, Plant Administrator of Salaried Personnel for the Colgate-Palmolive Company, Jersey City plant. This study was briefly described in the Number 3, 1958 *Supervisory Management Newsletter* of The American Management Association. A comparison was made of plant safety records for the nine-month period before the training program with a comparable period after the program. The frequency rate for lost-time accidents was measured along with the number of reported accidents. The frequency rate dropped from 4.5% to 2.9% and the number of reported accidents dropped from 41 to 32. This improvement was credited directly to the training effort because no physical changes were made which affected the accident rate.

At a 1958 Conference of The Management Institute, University of Wisconsin, Dr. G. Roy Fugal of the General Electric Company described a before-and-after evaluation of one of their safety programs. The purpose of the training was to reduce the number of accidents and to increase the regularity with which all accidents, major and minor, were reported. The training program consisted of the usual presentations, discussions, and movies which were very dramatic in describing accidents and their implications. The comprehensive evaluation indicated that the training program did not have desirable results. Therefore, a new approach to training was adopted which was more oriented to the job relationship between the foreman and each worker. An evaluation of this kind of safety training program did indicate the desired results.

Postal Carrier Training

In the September-October 1957 issue of the *Journal of the ASTD,* John C. Massey described a program in which he evaluated in terms of results. Experimental group "A" received 35 hours of orientation training under the post office training and development program. A comparable group called control group "B" did not receive any training. Results of this study are shown in Table I on the following page.

The design of this evaluation study includes an experimental as well as a control group. The importance of using these was emphasized in Part 3 of this series. It should also be used in evaluating results wherever possible to overcome the difficulty described by Dr. Keachie.

TABLE I
RESULTS OF TRAINING

| Category | *Total Number of Incidents* | |
	Experimental Group "A"	*Control Group "B"*
Negligent Accidents	5	8
Misdeliveries	21	33
Mishandling Valuable Mail	3	7
Late Reporting	35	32
Absence Without Reporting	3	6
Abuse of Sick Leave	8	12
Errors in Relay Operations	13	22
Adverse Probationary Reports	4	9
Discourtesy	4	5

An Insurance Company Study

In a recent letter, S. W. Schallert of the Farmers Mutual Insurance Company of Madison, Wisconsin reported to me on an evaluation he had made. A number of their claims adjustors were enrolled in the Vale Technical Institute of Blairsville, Pennsylvania. The purpose of the three-week course was to improve the ability of adjustors to estimate and appraise automobile physical damage.

The specific technique used by Schallert was to have the adjustors keep track of their savings for approximately six months after returning from Vale. These savings were the difference between the estimate of damage by garages and the estimate of damage by the claims adjustors who had been trained at Vale. Where the final cost of the adjustment was the same as the estimate made by the Farmers Mutual man, this was considered the savings.

In other words, the purpose of the training was to prepare the adjustors to make estimates which they could justify and sell. Actual dollars and cents figures could then be used to determine whether or not the cost of sending these adjustors to Vale was justified.

A Cost Reduction Institute

Several years ago, two graduate students at the University' of Wisconsin attempted to measure the results' of a "Cost Reduction Institute" conducted by The Management Institute of the University. Two techniques were used. The first was to conduct depth interviews with some of the supervisors who had attended the course and with their immediate superiors. The other technique was to mail questionnaires to the remaining enrollees and to their supervisors. Following is a brief summary of that study:

A. DEPTH INTERVIEWS

Interview With Trainees

1. Have you been able to reduce costs in the few weeks that you have been back on the job?

    Replies:

    13 men - yes

    3 men - no

2 men - noncommittal or evasive

1 man - failed to answer

2. How? What were the estimated savings?

Different types of replies indicated that the thirteen people who said they had made cost reductions had done so in different areas. But their ideas stemmed directly from the program, according to these trainees.

Interview of Superiors

Eight of the cost reduction actions described by the trainees were confirmed by the immediate superior and these superiors estimated total savings to be from $15,000 to $21,000 per year. The specific ideas that were used were described by superiors as well as by the trainees.

B. MAILED QUESTIONNAIRES

Questionnaires were mailed to those trainees who were not contacted personally. The results on the questionnaire were not nearly as specific and useful as the ones obtained by personal interview. The study concluded that it is probably better to use the personal interview rather than a questionnaire to measure this kind of program.

Employee Relation Index (ERI)

In the December 1955 issue of *The Harvard Business Review,* Willard V. Merrihue of General Electric Company and Raymond A. Katzell of Richardson, Bellows, Henry and Company described a very complex approach. According to them, "measuring performance is essential if we are to know whether the planning, the organizing, and all the other functions which preceded logically and time wise are, in fact, being discharged as well as they could or should be." The ERI is designed to measure the extent to which groups of employees accept and perform in accordance with the objectives and policies of the company. The following indicators constituted the ERI: (1) periods of absence; (2) separations; (3) initial visits to the dispensary for occupational reasons~ (4) suggestions submitted through the suggestion system; (5) actions incurring disciplinary suspension; (6) grievances submitted through the formal grievances procedures; (7) work stoppages; and (8) participation in the insurance plan.

At the time this article was written by Merrihue and Katzell, the ERI was in its preliminary stages. Also, it did not deal directly with evaluating training programs although it indicated it might be used as a measurement yardstick. The article in its entirety should be read by those persons who are interested in the complex area of measuring training programs in terms of results. Several practical ideas might be obtained which will be helpful in establishing specific evaluation criteria and procedures.

Measuring Organizational Performance

Another sophisticated and penetrating article related to evaluation was written by Rensis Likert. It appears in the March-April 1958 issue of *The Harvard Business Review.* It shows how changes in productivity can be measured on a before and after basis. Two different types of groups were used; the first was a group of supervisors trained in using a democratic kind of leadership in which decision making involved the participative technique. The supervisors in the other group were trained· to make their own decisions and not ask subordinates for suggestions.

In addition to measuring the results in terms of productivity, such factors as loyalty, attitudes, interest, and work involvement were also measured. Where both training programs resulted in positive changes in productivity, the "participative" approach resulted in better feelings, attitudes, and other human relations factors.

The article described another excellent study from the University of Michigan. Dr. Likert concluded by saying that "industry needs more adequate measures of organizational performance than it is now getting."

Summary

And so we see that the evaluation of training programs in terms of "results" is progressing at a very slow rate. Where the objectives of training programs are as specific as the reduction of accidents, the reduction of grievances, and the reduction of costs, we find a number of attempts have been made. In a few of them, the researchers have attempted to segregate factors other than training which might have had an effect. In most cases, the measure on a before and after basis has been directly attributed to the training even though other factors might have been influential.

Studies like those of Merrihue-Katzell and Likert attempt to penetrate the difficulties encountered in measuring such programs as human relations, decision making, and the like. In the years to come, we will see more efforts along this direction and eventually we may be able to measure human relations training, for example, in terms of dollars and cents. At the present time however, our research techniques are not adequate.

Conclusion

One purpose of these four articles has been to stimulate training directors to take a penetrating look at evaluation. It has been emphasized that their future and the future of their training programs depends to a large extent on their ability to evaluate and to use evaluation results.

The second objective has been to suggest procedures, methods, and techniques for evaluating training programs. A training director should begin by measuring in terms of results as described in Part 1 of this series. A second step should be to evaluate in terms of learning as described in Part 2. The third Part suggested ways and means of evaluating in terms of on-the-job behavior which should also be attempted. And finally this Part has analyzed some of the problems and approaches to measuring training programs in terms of its final objective-results.

It is hoped that the training directors who have read and studied these four articles are now clearly oriented on the problems and approaches to evaluating training. As future articles on evaluation appear, we training people should carefully analyze them to see if we can borrow the techniques and procedures the writers describe.

It is also hoped that as training directors evaluate their training programs, they will describe the procedures they have used and use this magazine and others to inform others of what they have done. Progress in the evaluation of training will result if all of us will freely exchange information on objectives, methods, and criteria.

Chapter 7

ഇരുങ്ങരു

Accolades for Kirkpatrick's Four Levels

"Kirkpatrick's four levels is the best I've ever seen in evaluating training effectiveness. It is sequentially integrated and comprehensive. It goes far beyond 'smile sheets' into actual learning, behavior changes and actual results, including long-term evaluation. An outstanding model!"

Stephen R. Covey
Author, *The 7 Habits of Highly Effective People* and *The Leader in Me*

"Don Kirkpatrick and his 4 levels of evaluation continue to resonate with my clients. Their clarity and relevance open the door for a meaningful conversation about what I am expected to achieve.

Don's work set the standard for all of us evaluating our work."

Judith Hale, Ph.D., CPT
Director of Certification
ISPI

"Hundreds of thousands of trainers use Don Kirkpatrick's Four Levels of Evaluation worldwide. Rich in simplicity, brilliantly practical, Don's Four Levels are as relevant today as they were a half-century ago when he first introduced them.

Does that mean that the Father of Learning Evaluation has been sitting back resting on his laurels? Oh no! Even though the Four Levels were nearly perfect at their inception, over the years, as the field of training evolved, so did Kirkpatrick's model. The evaluation guru honed his expertise and modernized his evaluation model to a smooth step-by-step process worthy of the best 21st century trainers.

So whether you conduct classroom training, online learning, or one-on-one coaching, this is the essential tool for all practitioners! If you aren't using the Four Levels, you aren't evaluating!"

    Elaine Biech
    Author, *Business of Consulting, Training for Dummies, ASTD Handbook for Workplace Learning Professional*

"As ASTD CEO and Executive Director during the early growing years of the society, Don Kirkpatrick was one of my favorite volunteer Presidents.

I remember so well, and with great fondness, the first time Don and I appeared on an ASTD International Conference stage--in Las Vegas, a thousand years ago, when we delivered an upbeat and entertaining general session presentation entitled, Futurethink: Training and Development ...Where Do We Go from Here?

We had some contemporary answers to share at the time, but what is especially special about Don is that he is still asking the same question, and is always ready with fresh answers and ideas.

How lucky our profession is to have Don grace our stage--then and now-- through the years!"

    Kevin O'Sullivan
    President
    The O'Sullivan Group, Inc.

"Congratulations on the 50th anniversary of the Four Levels. I have been amazed by the impact your work has had on training professionals all over the world. Thank you for being an inspiration to me so that I entered the field of training and development and have stayed in it for 20 years.

May you continue to see the fruits of your labor, and may God continue to bless you. With love from your daughter, Sue."

> Sue Muehlbach
> Manager, Sales Training and Performance Development
> Delta Air Lines

"Don's work has had significant impact on the way that the UK Armed Forces delivers its training. Within the UK Defence Systems Approach to Training, Kirkpatrick's Four Levels form the foundation of the evaluation phase of training, and have done so for many years.

In the face of many alternative approaches to evaluation, the UK military's continuous endorsement of the Kirkpatrick approach is indicative that – though 50 years old – the Four Levels still add value to the measurement of training's impact on operations. Though many attempt to decry their validity in the 21st century, the 4 levels have remained a basically simple tool but with real impact.

There are not many theoretical approaches that have both survived for half a century and have had a measurable impact on the real world – the anniversary of the Kirkpatrick Four Levels is something to celebrate."

> Wing Commander Al Thomas
> Training Policy
> Royal Air Force

"If there is one thing for which I will always be grateful to Don, it is his constant reminder to make sure that the measurement and evaluation strategy is fully aligned with the organization's goals and strategies. By having that alignment all the way up the organization it makes executing the Four Levels almost effortless.

When your measurement and evaluation strategy is in alignment with the business strategy, chances of being questioned on the validity of your results should drop dramatically. To remain viable, training organizations must have that validity in the eyes of their business stakeholders."

Michael Woodard
Director, Georgia Pacific University
Georgia-Pacific Consumer Products

"It is not often these days that one gets to commemorate an event that happened 50 years ago, within our own life spans. I doubt that Don Kirkpatrick had any idea of the impact his word and ideas would have on the business of training in general. For our firm, Don's ideas are the basis for founding the business we enjoy today. The Kirkpatrick Four Levels continue to be the standard across government and much of industry. A quick reading of the new Federal OPM Guidelines for Human Capital Assessment and Accountability (HCAAF) disclose the presence of Don's influence in the Continuous Learning section of that document. Private industry continues to view the Four Levels as the starting point for any effort to assess training effectiveness.

All of this proves that ideas don't have to be "new" to be effective. Not if they work, make sense, and are understandable. The Four Levels are all of that. We like to tell our training clients "conducting training without evaluation is like flying without instruments". It turns out that the same Four Levels to evaluate training have contained all along the formula for positioning training to contribute meaningfully to business success by helping to understand why, what, when and how we should train! All along, Don has been telling us that the Four Levels come into play *before* the first learning objective is ever put to paper.

We are grateful for Don's work and contributions. We look forward to the next 50 years! Congratulations, Don!"

Ronald Meyer
PTG International

"How do we evaluate the usefulness of training? Or in current terms, how do we ensure training can add value to the bottom line? However the question maybe framed, Don Kirkpatrick addressed the question of the usefulness of training with his simple four level evaluation framework 50 years ago.

Don's impact on the industry has been so huge that every organization attempting to assess the value of training uses his four level model. Not a single discussion on training evaluation takes place without reference to it. His ideas were so brilliantly simple that everyone attempting to demonstrate the value of training could use them.

Don is an outstanding professional, with extraordinary communicative energy and passion. He has delivered the most powerful, insightful and thought-provoking ideas to add value to training.

What differentiates Don from the other gurus is his selfless approach to contribution. His openness to sharing his knowledge with the world is without parallel."

R. Palan Ph.D. A.P.T.
Chairman & CEO
SMR Group

"In 1994, I was designing a training intervention for a big company and one of the goals was to develop some metrics for training. I talked to a friend who suggested I search for the Kirkpatrick Model, unknown at that time in Colombia.

The same year I was planning to go the ASTD International conference and went to Don's class. I bought a video and a book, and invited Don to do a workshop in Colombia. Since then we have done various workshops in Colombia on the model, and we know the Kirkpatrick Model is being used in big companies in our country.

In meeting Don, besides knowing the model, I learned that in order to teach you have to have his energy, conviction, love, and enthusiasm."

Germán A. París
President
PyB Su Socio en capacitación

"When I was a young trainer in the 1960's, I had the good fortune to read Don Kirkpatrick's articles about Training and Development evaluation. At that time, I didn't know much about evaluation other than the trainees were supposed to like the session. The Four Levels hit me like a bolt. Of course, there was more than a single way to conduct an evaluation.

Over the years I have gone back to Don's theory over and over again with the comfort that if I did my best to use it, I could be pretty well assured that I would end up with a clear picture of what my training efforts were accomplishing. Today the Four Levels seems fundamental to the success of our profession."

Rollin Glaser, Ed.D.
Chairman
HRDQ

"We are delighted to be long-term partners with Drs. Don and Jim Kirkpatrick. This relationship makes a huge impact on professional development of HR representatives in Russia. The training participants (representatives of more than 50 global and Russian companies) highly appreciate the solid structure, coherence and applicability of the 4 level system.

On a personal note, I must say that I admire Don Kirkpatrick for the ability to create something that has been working for the last 50 years, and Jim for adapting and promoting the methodology globally."

Svetlana Chumakova
MCC, Executive & Corporate Coach, Mentor -Coach
President of ICF Chapter - Russia

NOW: BEYOND THE FOUR LEVELS

This section of the book focuses on the true intent of the Kirkpatrick Four Levels and the latest thinking about the model:

- The Five Kirkpatrick Foundational Principles
- The Kirkpatrick Business Partnership Model^{SM}
- A Call to Action

Chapter 8

Kirkpatrick Foundational Principle #1

The End is the Beginning

At the beginning of 2009 we defined the five Kirkpatrick Foundational Principles. These describe the elements of the model that have always been "in there", but tend to be misunderstood or unused. The following chapters define each of the principles in more detail and provide practical guidance for using the Kirkpatrick Model fully and successfully. For a short summary of each of each principle, refer to the Resources section of this book.

Kirkpatrick Foundational Principles

1. The End is the Beginning
2. *Return on Expectations*^{SM} (*ROE*^{SM}) is the Ultimate Indicator of Value
3. Business Partnership is Necessary to Bring About Positive ROE
4. Value Must be Created Before it Can Be Demonstrated
5. A Compelling *Chain of Evidence*^{SM} Demonstrates Your Bottom Line Value

Kirkpatrick Foundational Principle #1 is "The End is the Beginning". Similar to the Kirkpatrick Four Levels, this principle is elegant in its simplicity. We believe that most people inherently know that at the start of any initiative it is wise to think about what ultimate result is desired, and make sure that all involved agree on that result. We also know that this type of thought and discussion doesn't always occur before action begins.

To start a project with business value in mind, first consider what Level 4 Results you seek. To make this point, we have inverted the diagram of the Kirkpatrick Four Levels to show Level 4 first:

Kirkpatrick Four Levels

Level 4: Results	To what degree targeted outcomes occur, as a result of the learning event(s) and subsequent reinforcement.
Level 3: Behavior	To what degree participants apply what they learned during training when they are back on the job.
Level 2: Learning	To what degree participants acquire the intended knowledge, skills, and attitudes based on their participation in the learning event.
Level 1: Reaction	To what degree participants react favorably to the learning event.

As stated earlier, "The End is the Beginning", like all of the foundational principles, is not actually anything new. Rather, it is a clarification for those who have misunderstood the Kirkpatrick Model and how to properly use it. On page 26 of *Evaluating Training Programs: The Four Levels* (1st Edition, Berrett-Koehler, 1994), Don Kirkpatrick wrote:

> "Trainers must begin with desired results and then determine what behavior is needed to accomplish them. Then trainers must determine the attitudes, knowledge, and skills that are necessary to

bring about the desired behavior(s). The final challenge is to present the training program in a way that enables the participants not only to learn what they need to know but also to react favorably to the program."

This distinguishes the development of the plan to build, deliver, and evaluate effective programs (which start with Results), from the actual data collection and presentation of the *Chain of Evidence*^{SM} (which *do* begin with Level 1). In other words, on the front end of a program during the planning stage, the model should be used upside down, starting with determining the desired Level 4 Results. Then, when the program is being executed and will actually be evaluated, the levels are followed in sequential order starting with Level 1. So the majority of the time, the model is used upside down, starting with Level 4.

Redefining Training Effectiveness

The good news is that the misconceptions regarding proper use of the Kirkpatrick Model are quite easily remedied. Training professionals who wish to increase their effectiveness need to become business-minded and start with Level 4. Being training-minded is not enough. We must become true strategic business partners. To do so we must redefine the definition and role of training, as well as training effectiveness. "Training effectiveness" can no longer be the number of people who show up to training, the volume of courses we offer, the size of our budget, or ratings we get on our smile sheets. Rather, it needs to be defined as the degree to which we help to accomplish the objectives set forth by and negotiated with our key business stakeholders.

> **Key business stakeholder:** A member of the corporate jury that has a stake in the success outcomes of a training initiative, and ultimately judges the value of training relative to its costs.

The first step in following Kirkpatrick Foundational Principle #1 is to determine what our key business stakeholder expectations are for our efforts. A question we like to ask to start this conversation is, "What will success look like to you?" The response to that question is the beginning of what we must accomplish as strategic business partners.

> **"What will success look like?":** The cornerstone question that helps convert generic stakeholder expectations into observable, measurable success outcomes, which subsequently become the Level 4 targets of ROE

Jim once had a client with a chain of hospitals that wanted to improve their results. Senior leaders decided to name their initiative, "Drive to Excellence". So they ran it up the flagpole (literally) and unified the company behind this program. They brought in Jim to help design the training and evaluation.

One of the first things Jim did was ask them the all-important question, "What will success look like?" They weren't sure. He asked a different way: "What does excellence mean, and how will you know when you have accomplished it?" Their response was, "We'll know it when we see it". Jim pressed on, and scheduled individual meetings with each of the company leaders. What resulted was a list of different "results" being sought from each of the leaders and their respective business units.

Collectively the organization was not clear on what their initiative was supposed to accomplish. Jim was not about to sign up for designing a training program around either a vaguely stated goal or a completely divergent list of non-shared goals. You shouldn't either. Clearly defining the target and focus of an initiative is the necessary first step to being able to meet it.

Getting to the True Business Result

Often when we have a conversation about program goals with clients, we find that the business stakeholders try to answer the question in training terms. Whether they are trying to relate to us or "dumb it down" is unclear. But we do know that a response to this question phrased in training terms is not the response we seek, and not one you should be satisfied with either. It may take a few additional questions to peel back the layers to get to the true business result being sought that the training needs to support.

The next questions you will likely have to ask your business stakeholders to clarify their vision are things like, "In order to what?" or "So that you can do what?"

"In order to what?": An important question asked during preliminary conversations defining the goals of a training initiative that helps move from training-centric to true business outcomes.

Here is a brief example of what that might look like:

Alan (training professional): *Hi Sue. You mentioned you would like some training support for your new product launch. What did you have in mind?*

Sue (marketing professional): *Yes. We need all the salespeople to know the new product inside and out.*

Alan: *Of course. Tell me, when you say "know the product inside and out", what would a successful training program deliver in that regard?*

Sue: *Good question. I am thinking that they will be able to confidently tell a customer about all of the product features and benefits.*

Alan: *Got it. One more question. If the salespeople are able to do that, what type of results do you think that might produce?*

Sue: *We are expecting a quick ramp-up for sales. We need this product to be in our top ten sellers by the end of the year.*

Alan: *Wow. That's a big goal. When do you want to get together to talk about the training plan...*

It may take you a few more questions than it took Alan to get the information you need. In this conversation with Sue, he ascertained that her Level 4 Result is to have sales of the new product in the top ten by the end of the year. She thought that the way they would do this is to have salespeople share the features and benefits with customers (Level 3). To do that, they would clearly need to know the features and benefits (Level 2), and be engaged in the training enough to learn what they needed to know (Level 1).

What do you suppose would happen if Alan had taken Sue's first response and ran with it? If all he knew is that the salespeople should "know the product inside and out", he would miss the mark in the training he creates. By asking a few more questions and finding out the ultimate business result Sue seeks, Alan is able to continue to ask important questions to ensure he designs training materials that will meet the stated needs. More importantly, he has an idea of what type of support, reinforcement, encouragement, and monitoring will be needed after the training so the desired behaviors are performed and the results are hopefully attained.

It is important to note that it is not only business leaders who sometimes can't see past the training activities when discussing desired outcomes. Your own colleagues in learning and development may have trouble with this as well. We conducted a two-day seminar recently and at the end, we had everyone state where they thought they stood before the seminar, and what their goals would be afterwards. Nearly everyone, to our delight, phrased their goals in terms of how they would partner with, support, and connect themselves to the business as much as possible. One training manager said he was going to work on improving his training programs. This was not exactly the level of thinking we were hoping for.

An Equally Important Question

A less frequent, yet equally important, spin on this principle is to also identify, "what failure will look like." In other words, what might the costs of non-action (or poorly executed action) be for the initiative and the company? In this case, what if they conducted no sales training and put the product out in the market? What are the chances it would become the best seller they are counting on? Comparing the costs of action to inaction can be a valuable calculation when determining where to allocate a limited training budget.

While foundational principle #1 is quite simple, we are not suggesting that it is easy to accomplish. We can't just go to our jury members (our business partners) with a blank tablet and ask them, "What are your business needs, your expectations for training, and ultimately what success will look like?" Most of the time they do not know, haven't thought through it yet (as the previous example illustrates), or have unrealistic expectations for what training can deliver. Finding out what the jury expects is usually a process involving many questions, and perhaps a few separate conversations.

Once there is agreement on what success looks like and the "needles" on the "dashboard" that need to be moved, we can address how to bring about true value to our organizations or clients, and convince our juries of the ultimate value of our efforts. Working in this order creates the best chance of training, and ultimately business, success. The more clearly the success outcomes are defined in the beginning the better the resources and efforts can be targeted to them. This makes hitting the target easier and much more likely. Which leads us to the next chapter and Kirkpatrick Foundational Principle #2: *Return on Expectations*^{SM} (*ROE*^{SM}) is the ultimate indicator of value.

Chapter 9

Kirkpatrick Foundational Principle #2

Return On Expectations^{SM} (*ROE*^{SM}) is the Ultimate
Indicator of Value

Kirkpatrick Foundational Principle #2 is "Return On Expectations (ROE) is the ultimate indicator of value". If we don't get this one right, over the next few years the training industry as we know it may become extinct. Training professionals need to be able to bring value to the business, and then demonstrate that value.

> **Return on Expectations**^{SM} **(ROE**^{SM}**):** What a successful training initiative delivers to key business stakeholders demonstrating the degree to which their expectations have been satisfied.

Your Corporate Jury Defines Your Value

Our corporate jury judges our value, so we need to know what they expect of us, deliver it, and then be able to show that we did. We call this concept Return On Expectations (ROE). We firmly believe it is the best way to demonstrate the value of our training and reinforcement efforts. Why? Because it always presents bottom line results and value in words and numbers that are the most meaningful to our customers – our business stakeholders – because *they defined them in the first place.*

Corporate Jury: The individual or group of business partners who ultimately judge the degree to which training efforts add value to the business in relation to their costs. This group subsequently controls or influences training department budgets, staffing, and future.

Principle #2 is where training professionals must humbly accept the fact that they largely *support* initiatives; typically they do not *create* or *drive* them. Wendy worked in a training department in the past that would poll the business stakeholders on what they wanted, then systematically shoot down the requests and just do what they thought was right. This is a formula for training extinction. The role of the training group is to support the key business initiatives of a company. The key business stakeholders almost always drive those initiatives.

Define Your Jury

The first step in achieving stakeholder ROE is to determine just who makes up your jury in the first place. This is not always as obvious as it sounds. Consider all parties that will be interested in whether or not you produce positive results. This can include executives, managers, customers, and the training participants themselves. Through business partnership, define the key stakeholders whose expectations will be the most important for you to satisfy.

Business Partnership: Cooperative effort between the training department and other business and support units in the company.

Define What Evidence Is Needed

It is important to not only know what success will look like to your key business stakeholders, but how they want to see evidence for ROE. You can do this by asking them (and yourself) what it will take to convince them that the business value of your efforts exceeds the costs. From this information you can determine what "evidence" you will need to gather to make up what we call a compelling *Chain Of Evidence*[SM].

Chain of Evidence[SM]: Data, information, and testimonies at each of the four levels that when presented in sequence, act to demonstrate value obtained from a business partnership initiative.

This is where we build on the Level 4 Results we defined in the last chapter. Instead of charging forward once your jury has told you what success will look like, you must negotiate their stated expectations into measurable success outcomes. Your business stakeholders are experts in their fields, and you are an expert in yours. This conversation will leverage your mutual expertise to create a plan that will satisfy stakeholders and business needs, and be realistic and achievable for you, their training partners.

Here is what we mean by this. A common Level 4 Result that your business partners may seek is increased profitability. Simple enough. However, how would you define and measure it? One can increase profitability by increasing sales, reducing costs, raising prices, or any number of other ways. At this stage you need to talk (and in some cases negotiate) with your key business stakeholders for them to define what exactly you and they will measure to define Level 4 Results. If you determine that increased sales is what you will measure, then define how you will actually measure it. For example, is there a sales report that can be referenced?

It is also important at this stage for you to ensure that the success outcomes being requested are things you feel that training can support, and ultimately deliver. This is usually a question of scope and resources. For example, if the conversation in this scenario continues with stakeholders desiring an increase in sales, then suggesting that you should be able to accomplish this with one, stand-alone 30-minute elearning module, that's where the negotiation comes in. Using your training expertise, you may need to do some education and define what outcomes are reasonable for the time and resources available to invest in training and subsequent reinforcement. Or, discuss what additional resources will be needed to accomplish the outcome they seek.

Determine How You Will Present Your Evidence

Once you have defined with your key business stakeholders what success will look like, the specific outcomes they seek, and how they will be measured, the final consideration is how they wish to have the data presented to them. We also urge you to put thought into what data is the most important to your stakeholders when you present it.

We believe that training professionals are "on trial" right now. The training industry is continually, and rightfully, being judged by corporate juries as to whether or not training costs are in line with business value delivered. This is the same scrutiny and analysis that nearly every other business unit has been subject to all along, so this should not be unexpected or viewed as unfair. Members of your "jury" will ultimately decide the fate of your training programs, and perhaps your job, based on your real and perceived value.

The charge that training does not always deliver as much value as it should relative to its cost is founded in many cases. One reason is that we typically start an initiative with training (Levels 1 and 2), not with ultimate business results (Level 4) in mind. We often see application of the four levels as, "smile sheets, pre and post-tests, and hope for the best". This reflects the reality that many training professions work only in their comfort area – Levels 1 and 2 – and never get to the critical levels that truly demonstrate meaningful value to our business stakeholders – Levels 3 and 4.

Getting Past Level 2

Research data varies in terms of how many training initiatives get measured beyond Level 2. According to the *2005 ASTD State of the Industry Report*, 91 percent of all learning events are measured at least to Level 1. According to a 2000 McMurrer survey of the ASTD Benchmarking Forum, only 13 percent of organizations use Level 3, and 3 percent Level 4 evaluation. So while there is quite a lot of evaluation happening, the majority seems to be at Levels 1 and 2. Few are getting to Level 3, and fewer yet to Level 4 to connect the learning initiative to organizational objectives.

In defense of training professionals everywhere, it is somewhat easy to understand why many of them don't currently get past Level 2. Whoever applied the "levels" to Don's four words started with Level 1 as Reaction. Had the model been turned upside down in the first place, it would have saved many well-intended learning professionals from getting stuck at Level 2.

We are also not fond of depictions of the model that show it as a pyramid, with a large base labeled "Level 1", and a tiny triangle on the top called "Level 4". This again perpetuates the misguided tendency to evaluate all programs at Level 1, and evaluate a smaller and smaller number of them up to Level 4. These are all reasons why we now turn the model upside down and depict the four levels as equal in size.

Besides the typical depiction of the Kirkpatrick Model, there are at least three other reasons training professionals have trouble getting to Levels 3 and 4. See if you still cling to any of these antiquated, trainer-centric beliefs that will limit your success as a strategic business partner:

1. Much of the literature over the past two decades has suggested that people should first master Level 1 before moving on to Level 2, then master Level 2 before moving on to Level 3. While they usually have little

challenge getting beyond the reaction / smile sheets of Level 1, they frequently get bogged down at Level 2. This is mostly because they spend an inordinate amount of time, money, and effort perfecting the pre and posttests that training's roots in secondary education say we must do.

Instead of dealing with key issues of *usability* (for learning professionals) and *credibility* (for ultimately demonstrating value), they worry too much about *validity* and *reliability*. Don't get us wrong. There is nothing wrong with valid and reliable pre and posttests, *except* when they become more important than the needs dictate – or when they keep you from getting to the levels that are much more highly regarded by your business partners – Levels 3 and 4.

2. Levels 1 and 2 are easier to accomplish because they are within training control, meaning, they can be completed while we have the training participants in our presence. Generally Levels 1 and 2 don't require us to make business cases for involvement from supervisors, managers, and executives. It is easier to work among our 'own kind'.

    Aligned with this notion is the misguided belief that it is not the responsibility of the training professional or department to go beyond Level 2, since we have no *control* over what happens after the training is complete. It is true that we do not have the *authority* to direct employee development and performance, but it is our *responsibility* to make it as easy as possible for our business partners to execute this critical component of every initiative.

3. Training professionals have traditionally defined their value through the number of people that attend training

programs, scores on Level 1 reaction sheets, and the amount of learning that has occurred. All of these are important, yet only to the extent that they translate into Level 3 Behaviors on the job, and Level 4 Results that are key to the business.

More meaningful measures that training professionals should adopt are things like on-the-job execution of skills taught in training, and tracking of business metrics for the topic being trained, because training effectiveness needs to be defined beyond Levels 1 and 2 to be relevant to the business.

We have defined in the first two Kirkpatrick Foundational Principles that the end is actually the beginning, and ROE is the ultimate indicator of value. We now turn our attention to the third principle, which outlines another important element of delivering true business value: business partnership.

Chapter 10

Kirkpatrick Foundational Principle #3

Business Partnership is Necessary to Bring About Positive *ROE*^{SM}

Kirkpatrick Foundational Principle #3 is, "Business Partnership is Necessary to Bring About Positive ROE". We feel that again this is nothing terribly new. Perhaps by now it is even obvious to you. The unfortunate thing is that we don't often see it happening in organizations, so we feel it necessary to explain the importance of business partnership for producing ROE.

Wendy often gets after Jim for seeing training metaphors in everyday life. Sometimes every day! Here is an example that helps to illustrate Kirkpatrick Foundational Principle #3:

The other day we were watching *The Soloist* and decided to listen to the entire Beethoven symphony that was playing at the end of the movie. As the credits rolled by, we found ourselves discussing the many people that were involved in the production of a movie. We noted that they did not just list the actors in the credits, or even just the actors, director, and producers. *Everyone* who was even remotely involved in the making of the motion picture was listed, including "assistant key grips", "chauffeurs for the actors", "animal trainers", and "associate hair stylists."

We thought of how this concept applies to our own programs and initiatives. Trainers and line managers are co-directors. Training participants are the actors. Business sponsors are the executive producers. Trainers are the directors at the beginning of a "production" because they are the ones who help the actors (our training participants) to succeed through our training and participation in subsequent reinforcement. After training, the line managers take over the director role, heading up the encouragement, reinforcement, monitoring, and rewarding of key behaviors performed by the training participants. Your business sponsors and champions are the executive producers because they take care of the budget, approvals, contracts, etc.

Training Participants are the Real "Stars"

The training participants are the real stars, and the ones who should get the glory. We hope this does not surprise you. The training participants are the ones who need to learn what you teach, and then successfully apply it on the job. This is a much greater feat than our teaching of the class. In reviewing countless Level 1 reaction sheets, we think a few of you might have some thinking to do on this point. Does your reaction sheet contain leading questions that are intended to deliver accolades to you, the trainer? Or are the questions learner-centric, allowing your "stars" to indicate to what degree the course was helpful to them in preparing for a winning performance in their starring role back on the job?

This is all about giving credit where credit is due. There is overwhelming evidence that it takes more than training (Level 2) to achieve significant business results. Training events *in and of themselves* provide little hope to deliver positive, bottom line outcomes. Much has to happen *before* and *after* formal training in order to leverage actual learning. And learning professionals need help to do it. Our domain is Levels 1 and 2, which is one of the major reasons we spend almost all of our time there. But the actual *leverage and execution* of learning efforts and overall corporate strategy primarily occur at Level 3. The elusive Level 3 that is out of our control and frankly, out of our authority.

For all of these reasons, business partnership is necessary to produce the ROE that our stakeholders seek, which is fulfillment of the previously defined Level 4 outcomes and related measurements.

The Most Important Level

Colleagues often ask us two questions pertaining to the four levels: "Which are the most important?" and "Which are the most difficult to evaluate?"

Here is how we answer: The most important level to our business partners is Level 4. The most important level should be Level 3.   Therefore, the most important level for *training professionals* is Level 3.

The most difficult level to *evaluate* is Level 2 because of all of the validity and reliability issues. The most difficult level to *access* is Level 3 because of the challenge of getting our partners on board, and the level of effort required to create sustainability. By the way, the easiest level to evaluate is Level 4, because most often business areas or Human Resources are already collecting those metrics.

All of the above indicates the need for business partnerships. Not only do you need to call upon your business partners to help you identify what success will look like, but you need a cooperative effort throughout the learning and performance processes. Before training, learning professionals need to partner with supervisors and managers to prepare participants for training. Supervisors should explain to their direct reports what they will learn in training, why it's important, their expectations for actions during and after the training event, and the support they will receive in order to be successful. The attitude of training participants will likely be different if the event is prefaced this way by their direct supervisor.

Even more critical is the role of the supervisor or manager after the training. They are the key people who will reinforce newly learned knowledge and skills through support and accountability. This is why we feel they are the co-directors along with training professionals. The degree to which managers provide reinforcement and coaching on the job directly correlates to improved performance and positive outcomes. So this is critical to achieving positive ROE.

Support and Accountability: The two forces that need to be balanced after training in order to drive critical behaviors (see *Transferring Learning to Behavior,* 2005).

Other key business partners, akin to the others in movie credits, may include:

- Human Resources staff, as they make sure job descriptions, performance reviews, and incentives are aligned with targeted behaviors and success outcomes

- Information Technology, as they help us automate and streamline evaluation

- Marketing, as they help us promote and reinforce our efforts

- Administrative Assistants, as they help with logistics, data collection, and basically making it all work

Make A Business Case To Key Business Partners

Successful ROE does not occur unless you have built and leveraged partnerships. Crucial here is making business cases for all involved. This can be an easy sell if you clearly make the connection between training, their involvement, and the results they want to accomplish. All of your potential partners have "their own jobs to do" and are generally not looking for extra work. Your business case needs to show how your training, and their subsequent support and reinforcement, will help to deliver the business results that are most important to them.

Consider the following groups as candidates for which you will make a business case for business partnership and collaboration:

1. Your own training team: getting them to own the new definition of their role and industry that goes beyond design, develop, and deliver

2. Executives: sponsorship, endorsement, accountability for critical behaviors and drivers

3. Middle managers and other supervisors: coaching, development, and Level 3 and 4 evaluation

4. Other support areas – HR, IT, Marketing, etc.

5. Participants – ownership and personal responsibility

Surprisingly, do you know which group is often the most difficult to convince? Our own training colleagues. Do not just assume they are with you. Do not underestimate the power of and entrenchment in the traditional belief that training indeed ends when participants leave the classroom or turn off their computers.

Once you get the buy-in from the different groups, the execution or implementation of the principles of the *Kirkpatrick Business Partnership Model*SM is quite straightforward. Skipping the important process of building business partnerships will likely mean your initiative will fail or produce fewer results than it could. So we now turn our attention to how value will be created through these business partnerships in Kirkpatrick Foundational Principle #4: value must be created before it can be demonstrated.

Chapter 11

Kirkpatrick Foundational Principle #4

Value Must Be Created Before it Can Be Demonstrated

The Kirkpatrick Foundational Principle #4 states that, "Value must be created before it can be demonstrated". For those of you who are now convinced that the Kirkpatricks are masters of the obvious, you may be on to something. Again, we can hardly claim that this principle is new or visionary. It is neither of these things. It is another reminder to stay focused the ultimate result that an initiative has been designed to deliver, whatever that may be. If the initiative doesn't deliver value in the eyes of your business stakeholders, this puts the training group on shaky ground. So this chapter is dedicated to explaining how to provide maximum value.

Where Training Effectiveness Comes From

Research suggests that somewhere around 15 percent effectiveness can be expected from training events (Levels 1 and 2) alone. Around 50 percent comes from things that occur after training, when participants are back on the job (Level 3). So for training professionals to involve themselves only with the training event, they are making it difficult or impossible to be of true business value that is in line with their costs. Trying to demonstrate value that doesn't exist is similarly difficult.

Stated simply, Level 3 is where the majority of training value is created. So Level 3 is the critical place to focus attention in terms of supporting the creation of value, and then demonstrating what has occurred.

Besides improving programs and demonstrating their value, a lesser-known purpose of Kirkpatrick evaluation is to actually drive the application of on-the-job behaviors at Level 3 and subsequent Level 4 results. Why is Level 3 so often the "missing link", as we like to call it? Because training people typically own Levels 1 and 2, while the business is all consumed with Level 4. Therefore, Level 3 – the link, the bridge, and the magic – is most often left to fend for itself with no clear ownership or allocation of resources.

"The Missing Link": Another name for Level 3, because execution at this level is critical for maximizing Level 4 Results, yet neither training nor the business tends to take ownership for it.

This entire principle falls under the category of, "what gets measured matters, and gets done." Imagine if well-meaning participants graduate from well-meaning courses taught by well-meaning facilitators for well-meaning purposes. Then, after getting all excited about the investment their organization has made in their "professional development", and armed with new knowledge and skills, they get back to their jobs and *nothing is ever mentioned about it again*. Imagine their reactions – "I should have known – another flavor-of-the-month club initiative." You probably don't have to do much imagining to understand this scenario. It happens every day, and our guess is that you have at least once personally experienced it.

The gap between Levels 2 and 3 is real, and it happens all too frequently. We have come to call it "the great divide". Instead of finding indifference after training, imagine if training graduates were met by supervisors who say, "How was training? What did you learn? How can I help you implement it?" Imagine further if training graduates are given the chance to actually use what they learned, and encouraged to do so until it becomes business as usual. Imagine if they are shown that the new skills they are applying might provide them with a broader, deeper skill set that will help them advance in the organization. Imagine what would happen if your organization was filled with employees at all levels that view training as an opportunity to learn, apply, and contribute.

"The Great Divide": The significant gap that exists between Level 2 Learning and 3 Behavior, both in research correlation studies and actual practice.

This would, of course, take a lot of work, primarily in the form of good planning, monitoring and follow-up. Don and Jim wrote a book in 2005 called *Transferring Learning to Behavior*. In it, principles and practical tips are detailed to encourage this transfer, including monitoring, encouraging, reinforcing, and developing accountability systems that will compel training program graduates to actually apply what they learned.

Much of our own work is spent at Level 3 on these issues, as we find that positive efforts here act as force multipliers and maximize the investments made by our business stakeholders – our juries. Jim worked as the Training Director for First Indiana Bank in Indianapolis from 1997 to 2005. He spent most of his time with supervisors, managers, and executives encouraging them to actively coach and support their employees after training events. He found that this was the best use of his time, knowing that the good training his staff was delivering was only as good as the reinforcement that followed.

Why such an emphasis on what happens before and after training? A 2006 ASTD study on the causes of "training failure" (that is, training failing to meet predetermined objectives) found that the majority of failures occur on the job, after training has been completed.

This data is significant because it tells us that a relatively good job is being done with the areas we are comfortable in – designing, developing, and delivering training. It also tells us that if training is relied upon to create significant value, forget it. It is clear that the industry must get beyond the tradition of comfort, and enter an era of value – Levels 3 and 4. In short, reinforcement, accountability, and Level 3 evaluation will significantly increase the transfer of learning to behavior, which will significantly increase your bottom line impact, and correspondingly your value to the organization.

Causes of Training Failure

- 20 percent: lack of preparation before training
- 10 percent: faulty training methods in design, development, and delivery
- 70 percent: lack of management support and accountability, or opportunity to use what was learned in training soon enough on the job for the learning and behaviors to stick

2006 ASTD Study

The successful execution and ultimate value of any training program are, of course, contingent on excellent training events of all types. This is verified by positive engagement of learners (Level 1) and actual acquisition of targeted knowledge, skills, and attitudes (Level 2). We are often criticized for casting Levels 1 and 2, and even training, in a negative light. On the contrary, we believe they are the cornerstones of success. An effective training development methodology and supportive competencies are of foundational importance. They are not, however, the end, as we often treat them. (If you have an excellent competency management system that stops at Level 2 we would suggest you apply the concepts in this book and modify it).

We strongly urge you to secure or redeploy resources for critical programs to Level 3 efforts whenever you can. You can do this by identifying programs and initiatives that do not directly contribute to strategic business goals, and minimizing evaluation and reinforcement for those programs, moving precious resources to where you can really multiply strategic efforts and value.

How to Create Training With Business Value

The first half of this chapter is our emphatic plea to all training professionals to realize and embrace the power of Level 3 for learning effectiveness and value. Now we turn our attention to what learning professionals can actually do to ensure that Level 3 is leveraged. We left off in chapter 9 with the process for determining success outcomes (Level 4) with your key stakeholders. Once you know what outcomes you are trying to accomplish, the next important consideration is the critical behaviors (Level 3) that the training graduates will have to consistently perform on the job to support them.

Mastering involvement in and influence over Level 3 is the key to training success. If you can do this, you will differentiate yourself from most other training professionals and produce business results that will make you valuable to your organization or clients. Wendy likes to say, "it's all about Level 3", because when it comes to success in the field of training, it is.

The process of defining the required critical behaviors is similar to how you determined the success outcomes: you ask your stakeholders, and negotiate the final determination. In this case, you are probably talking to the managers or supervisors who work with the intended training participants daily. Armed with the desired success outcomes, ask them what specific behaviors, if performed by their team members on a regular basis, would support and most likely deliver the desired success outcomes. The key here is that specific, observable, and measurable behaviors must be defined.

Critical behaviors: The few, key behaviors that employees will have to consistently perform in order to bring about the targeted outcomes.

Required organizational drivers must also be identified at this point. They are every bit as important as critical behaviors for success at Level 3. Required drivers can be defined as processes and systems that reinforce monitor, encourage, or reward performance of critical behaviors on the job.

Required drivers: Processes and systems that reinforce monitor, encourage, or reward performance of critical behaviors on the job.

Required Driver Examples

- Job aids

- Incentives for meeting goals

- Coaching and reinforcement

- Follow-up reminders after training

- Dashboards showing key behavior tracking

Necessities for success – prerequisite items, events, conditions, or communications that help head off problems before they get the chance to reduce the impact of an initiative, should also be addressed at this point. You can think of these as the larger, organizational level issues that need to be addressed before a program starts so that it has the best possible chance of succeeding.

Necessities for success: Prerequisite items, events, conditions, or communications that help head off problems before they reduce the impact of an initiative.

Necessities for Success Examples

- Communications related to the upcoming initiative

- Integration of critical behaviors into the performance appraisal process and job descriptions

- Visible management and executive support of and involvement in the initiative

Once the critical behaviors, required drivers, and necessities for success have all been defined and agreed upon, then (and only then) can you move on to designing the training program. Since there are many resources available on instructional design, and this is not typically where the problems with training effectiveness lie, we will cover this briefly.

Level 2: Designing the Training Program

The most important thing to remember as you design the training is to keep it focused on preparing participants to perform the critical behaviors when they are back on the job. This actually makes the instructional design process easier because it is very focused and streamlined. Avoid the temptation to add more to the class than is needed. Write the learning objectives to align with the desired behaviors, and limit the course content to accomplishing the objectives. This type of laser-focus will not only save time and money, it will increase your value in the eyes of your business stakeholders because it demonstrates good business sense.

Also consider what modality will best teach the learner how to perform the required behavior. An extreme example of this is the old training analogy, would you trust a pilot to fly a plane if he or she had completed only written exams to become certified to fly? If what you are teaching requires skill performance, make sure you have a hands-on skill check or at least a simulation as part of the training program.

Build Evaluation Elements into the Training Program

As you build the training program, weave in elements of evaluation along the way. Facilitators should be able to explain to participants the importance of what they are learning, how it is to be applied on the job, and what methods will be used to support and measure it during and after class. Reminding participants what is expected of them after class sets the stage for good learning during class and execution of key behaviors afterwards. It is also important to inform participants what will be measured and how, so there is no surprise or discomfort as a result. It is important to do this in the spirit of caring and helpfulness.

Make sure that Level 3 support is as integrated into your training program as possible. For example, have the facilitator introduce key job aids, and have participants use them to complete activities during class. During the instructional design process, go ahead and design any follow-up communication and refreshers you plan to use. You could even consider having participants register for "lunch and learn" or other refresher training events if you plan to hold them. Turn the "old" style trainer objection that, "we only have control at Levels 1 and 2", into "We have great control at Levels 1 and 2, so we will leverage that time to make the most impact we can at Levels 3 and 4".

Keep in mind that the Kirkpatrick Four Levels reflect more than an *evaluation* plan. When you get to Level 3 you also want to consider which drivers need top support, reinforcement, and rewards in terms of what you plan. Again, you want to build as much of that into your training program as possible so these things are ready and in place when training participants have completed the class. This will be greatly appreciated by the managers and supervisors who will be "passed the baton", if you will, when the training graduates return to the job and need to perform the behaviors they just learned about.

Keep the evidence your jury wants to see (and in what form) in mind as you design the course. It's good practice to build any necessary evaluation or tracking tools during the instructional design process to ensure that they complete, and fully align with the objectives. How many times have we heard training professionals on the evening before the launch of a new class, say, "Oops, I forgot to make my reaction sheet". Leaving evaluation methods as afterthoughts like this will not support ROE.

Make sure during the design and development of the program you sketch out your intended Chain of Evidence. Make sure you would believe it if it was presented to you. Share the concept with your key stakeholders and find out if they will believe it if you indeed are able to deliver it to them. Better to find out in the development stage if your evidence is going to be credible to the jury or not!

Key Questions To Ask

Here is a summary of the key questions to ask at each of the Four Levels when planning your training program. Use the answers to guide the design and contents of your training program.

Key Questions to Ask at Each Kirkpatrick Level

Level 4

- What will success look like?
- What evidence is needed?
- How will success be measured?

Level 3

- What critical behaviors will training graduates need to consistently perform on the job to bring about targeted outcomes?
- What are the required organizational drivers?
- What necessities for success exist within the organization?

Key Questions to Ask at Each Kirkpatrick Level

Level 2

- What do training participants need to learn to be able to perform the required on-the-job behaviors?

Level 1

- What learning environment and methods are appropriate for what needs to be taught?

Staying focused on the business result will actually make the job of the instructional designer much easier because the scope and content of the class will be clearly defined from the start.

Cause and Effect Relationships

Keep in mind the following cause and effect relationships as you begin any initiative where training will be involved:

Relationship #1

The success outcomes (ROE) will largely be determined by the degree to which training graduates actually perform the critical on-the-job behaviors, which will largely be determined by the degree to which necessities for success and required drivers have been implemented and executed. Contrary to what happens in many cases today, the design, development, and delivery of training programs must support the drivers, necessities for success, and critical behaviors. Starting with training and then hoping Level 3 execution "just happens" usually doesn't work.

Relationship #2

The clearer expectations are, the more likely an individual, department, team, or organization will be to meet those expectations. ROE is something everyone can relate to conceptually. Everyone has expectations for their own performance. Ideally this helps people to focus their efforts on what is most important. And in the perfect world, if people do what is expected and do it well, they will be rewarded accordingly. This is the basis of effective performance reviews and performance management.

Relationship #3

The more closely your plan aligns to what your jury thinks is important, the better chance you have of being seen as successful. Your jury is the body that will rule you guilty or innocent of training expenditures exceeding the value you ultimately deliver. Ensure that your plan and the way you express the value of your training is in line with their expectations before you start the training.

We now turn our attention to the culmination of all training efforts: the resulting Chain of Evidence.

Chapter 12

Kirkpatrick Foundational Principle #5

A Compelling *Chain Of Evidence*^{SM} Demonstrates Your
Bottom Line Value

The Kirkpatrick Foundational Principle #5 is, "A compelling Chain of EvidenceSM demonstrates your bottom line value". The Chain of Evidence is how you will demonstrate the value of training to the business. We recommend that you always consider the Chain of Evidence for every training program. The level of complexity and formality depends on the size and importance of the training initiative.

Level 1	Level 2	Level 3	Level 4
Reaction	Learning	Behavior	Results

Chain of Evidence^{SM}

A full, formal presentation of the Chain Of Evidence to business executives is generally reserved for major initiatives or programs. In the interest of monitoring the usage of limited resources, a full, in-person presentation is not always needed. It is usually performed for skeptical business leaders who need to see clear evidence for the power of the business partnership model, or the value of a particular strategy-focused initiative. It should be reserved to show clients the value that their investment and everyone's efforts have brought. It should be done to generate powerful marketing stories. If done correctly, it can lead to untold opportunities, as long as your jury is convinced of your value.

For your more "everyday" training programs, your Chain of Evidence will be much simpler. It could be a matter of defining what business objective each of your classes supports, and ensuring that there are some items that address Level 3. (We are making the assumption here that you were already evaluating at Level 1, and have sound learning objectives and methods at Level 2, which statistically seems to be the case).

Types of Evidence

A Chain Of Evidence is about connecting the dots – relevant and powerful bits of evidence from each of the four levels. This is akin to what a good attorney does during his or her closing argument to the jury. The more important the "case" (i.e. initiative or program), the closer together the dots should be.

It is important to make a compelling case with the proper balance of data, information, and testimonies. We often run into people who believe that evaluation is not useful unless it is complex, and that numeric data is the only type of evidence that should be considered. We find that thinking to be arrogant and training-centered rather than a true attempt to demonstrate ROE. The proper mix of evidence typically includes:

1. Relevant Data – numbers that show evidence of impact or improvement at each of the four levels. This is akin to "expert witness" testimony in a civil court scenario.

These data are usually gathered through such methods as surveys, observation checklists, work review, quizzes and tests, case study exercises, borrowed metrics, and action plan accomplishments.

2. <u>Information (testimonials)</u> – words from satisfied participants and stakeholders that add richness to the data. Very few jury members will be impressed with numbers alone. This aligns with what attorneys call "weeping widows".

    These powerful stories are typically gathered using focus groups, questionnaires, interviews, and email requests.

3. <u>Compelling Explanations</u> – the evidence presented to the jury must tell a story of value. Connections, root causes, cause-and-effect explanations, outside variables, success enablers, and recommendations to improve future impact must be presented to the jury so they can clearly see the story of training leading to learning, leading to performance, leading to impact.

    These explanations are not collected; rather they arise from analysis and discussion around the intent of the initiative and the elements that go into accomplishing the targeted outcomes.

Borrowed metrics: Relevant level 4 success outcomes that training professions obtain from business or human resource departments in order to complete a chain of evidence.

Compiling Your Evidence

An important point to remember when gathering your evidence is the audience. Your jury, comprised of business professionals, is going to be most interested in evidence related to Level 3 performance of critical behaviors and Level 4 accomplishment of results.

A colleague of ours named Nick DeNardo has a good way to explain this. He calls data from Levels 1 and 2 "consumptive metrics", which more or less tell the story of cost to our internal customers and external clients. This includes the time, money, and resources employed to develop training programs, and have participants away from work to attend.

> **Consumptive Metrics:** Participant attendance, Level 1, and Level 2 data that attempt to show training value, but instead highlight the costs of training to the business.

When we use data and information from Levels 3 and 4, however, we are speaking the language of value. Nick calls these, "impact metrics" or "value metrics". At Levels 3 and 4, your measures are demonstrating the performance of behaviors that are critical, as defined by the jury members themselves early on in the development process. It then measures the most important level, Level 4 Results. This is the impact on the business; the reason you did the training program in the first place.

> **Impact Metrics:** Level 3 and Level 4 metrics, which constitute the most relevant measurements of training effectiveness to key business stakeholders.

Think about your last progress report or presentation. What did you present as your "results"? Did you talk about the number of training participants, number of sessions held, and the wide variety of courses in your curriculum? When training professionals insist on using consumptive (Level 1 and 2) metrics like these to demonstrate their value alone, it is like putting bright red bull's-eyes on their backs and screaming, "Cut our budget!" Ensure that if you do present consumptive metrics, it is minimal in relation to impact metrics, and in support of the impact you have made on the business.

We believe that Level 1 and 2 evidence (data and testimonials) are a message of how good we are at what we do; Level 3 and 4 evidence tells the story of the good that we have done. Consider the implications of that!

The Dashboard: Monitoring Tool and Evidence Creator

Since we have defined that the evidence you are most interested in gathering is that to support Levels 3 and 4, we now introduce the concept of a dashboard. This is exactly what it sounds like: a highly visual display of the current levels of key measures so that everyone can see them at any given time.

Dashboard: A graphic depiction of key metrics in a business partnership initiative that monitors and communicates progress towards business outcomes. Typically color-coded in green, yellow, and red.

Consider developing a dashboard system to track and communicate the monitoring of key drivers, critical behaviors, and success outcomes within your organization. The "needles" on the dashboard visually show exactly where the organization is in the pursuit of the desired business outcomes.

"Needles": The Level 4 metrics a training initiative is designed to move, that will effectively demonstrate training value to key business stakeholders. This refers to a needle on a dashboard indicating the current level of a critical measurement.

In addition to capturing evidence of the impact of training, a dashboard also provides other benefits:

1. Early warning detection system- we like to use the analogy of a U.S. Air Force Airborne Warning and Control System (AWACS) plane. The Air Force uses this super expensive aircraft to extend air traffic control

radar beyond its normal reaches to see what is going on in a battle zone.

We want you to do the same for Level 3 critical behaviors and drivers on your own battlefield – in the trenches of everyday work. Your radar should be picking up the ongoing critical behaviors and drivers that are necessary to bring about success, and to be alerted to when things are not going as they should (the "warning" part), and to make necessary adjustments to bring them back to standards (the "control" part).

2. <u>Communication, reinforcement, and reassurance tool</u> - periodically send the dashboard to your jury members to reassure them that all is progressing well, and, except for unforeseen circumstances and variables, they can expect positive impact at Level 4. If possible, include some preliminary Level 4 metrics to provide additional confidence.

3. "<u>Derailer</u>" <u>warnings</u>- sometimes there are negative issues that jeopardize an initiative, and are beyond the scope of an individual or group. If and when you encounter this through your own AWACS system, enlist the power of the business partnership to solve it, based on prior agreed-upon accountability and intervention steps.

To illustrate this point, here is an example. Wendy worked for a consumer products company in the nineties that got the "consultant bug". For every problem in the company, they hired a consultant to solve it. The problem was, each department hired their *own* consultant. At the time, Wendy was heading a process change initiative that was intended to streamline and document business processes for the entire company. At the same time, however, there was a Six Sigma consultant working on manufacturing processes, and a relationship-oriented consultant working with the executive team on corporate communications. Wendy had to raise the red flag and say there were "too many cooks in the kitchen".

AWACS (Airborne Warning and Control System): A U.S. Air Force aircraft that monitors battlefield conditions and activity. Parallels the Kirkpatrick approach to continually monitoring and reporting on Level 3 activity.

Polish Your Presentation

It is sad when we see great training and reinforcement efforts go unrecognized because the leaders did not make a compelling case to their jury. This happens very frequently. No attorney in his or her right mind would think of handing a report to 12 jury members, asking them to read it, then eliciting questions, and asking them to render a judgment. Much of the power is in the presenting. So why would training professionals, when their jobs are "on trial", think anything other than a compelling presentation of the evidence to the jury would suffice?

Preparation is Critical

Jim has a good friend in Indianapolis who is an attorney named Don Murphy. He was a great resource for facts to support our upcoming book, *Training on Trial* (AMACOM, 2010). Don said that in the legal world, jury selection is taken very seriously. The attorneys on either side of a case do everything they can to find out about the jury members, and get the ones they think will vote in their favor if selected. In our world it would be unlikely we could actually choose our jury, but we like the idea of finding out everything you can about the jury members in advance so that you are prepared to make a case to which they will respond.

We also recommend you do a "dry run" of your final presentation for high impact, high potential programs. Practice the delivery of your compelling Chain of Evidence in front of a group of trusted people who understand the program. Get their reactions and allow them to provide feedback to hone your presentation. In our two-day Kirkpatrick Evaluation Certification program, we allow participants to practice presenting their business partnership model or evaluation plans to their fellow classmates. We are always impressed with the amount of learning that takes place during these sessions, and how enthusiastic and prepared the participants are to go back to their organizations and present their cases for real.

The Power of an Impact Study

The most effective way we know to demonstrate the bottom line value of your training is to conduct an impact study and present the findings. This can take a learning team from having to beg managers to release employees to attend training, to having managers ask for help with business needs, problems, and opportunities. Impact studies and jury presentations can transform you as an individual – consultant or organization professional – into a true strategic business partner.

If you are not familiar with impact studies, they involve selecting one or more key programs – key to strategy execution – and undertaking a robust training and evaluation effort to ultimately create and demonstrate value. The goal of an impact study is to show your corporate jury the power of the business partnership model in leveraging formal and informal training to maximize business impact. This impact is showcased to your business leaders in the terms and measures most meaningful to them, because you started with the question, "What will success look like to you (i.e. them)?"

While there are lots of steps involved in a comprehensive impact study, in a nutshell it involves selecting the right program(s), conducting effective training at Levels 1 and 2, reinforcing the learning at Level 3, and gathering evidence (data, information, and testimonials) all along the way to show the impact at Level 4.

An added benefit of a properly executed impact study is that it can easily serve as the pilot for developing a comprehensive training and evaluation methodology for all key programs in your organization.

Can you implement an impact study on your own? Sure you can. We have seen numerous organizations conduct impact studies with mixed success. Those that are unsuccessful are usually because their programs did not create many Level 4 Results in the first place, or their reports and story of value were not believed because they were prophets from their own country, if you will.

Finding Time and Resources to Evaluate

We are often asked, "How am I supposed to find the time and resources to evaluate programs at all four levels when I am already working overtime conducting training classes?" Here are some tips:

1. Ensure that you are focusing your time and effort on the programs that will produce the ROE your stakeholders have defined. If you have a gigantic catalog of classes, conduct analysis and map them to key company initiatives. If there are some that don't seem to fit, these are candidates to revamp or discontinue so that resources can be dedicated to mission-critical classes.

2. Scale the complexity of your evaluation to the size and importance of the initiative. Not every class you teach will require a formal report showing four levels of evaluation.

   For example, a class on your office email system might be measured with a five-question reaction sheet (Level 1), a hands-on activity during class (Level 2), a follow-up email asking for testimonials (Level 3), and a report from the company mainframe showing email usage statistics of program attendees before and after the class (Level 4). Measuring all four levels is not as complicated as some people make it seem.

In contrast, a major company initiative is the time to formally evaluate at all four levels with a business plan that is created hand-in-hand with stakeholders. Before the training occurs, check that the evaluation you plan to conduct (and corresponding evidence you will collect) will meet the needs of your corporate jury if you deliver it.

3. Use the business partnership approach in a broad way when looking at many individual training courses. For example, think about *all* courses related to new employee orientation as a unit. Discuss ROE and design your evaluation strategy for the entire grouping rather than each class individually.

Evidence of Your Value

In summary, your Chain of Evidence, if prudently gathered and expertly presented, can be just the information that will lead your jury to find you innocent of your costs exceeding your value to the business. And be sure to keep the jury attentive as "the credits roll by", and you properly recognize all of the people who were involved in the initiative. This shows that beyond a reasonable doubt, the business partnership model is the key to successful business execution.

In your everyday training programs, informally create a Chain of Evidence showing how each course connects to the key business objective, and how Level 3 is supported. Even if you aren't asked to present it, always think of your training in terms of the Level 4 business objectives it supports.

We now turn our attention to the Kirkpatrick Business Partnership Model, which is the embodiment of the five Kirkpatrick Foundational Principles and the Kirkpatrick Model.

Chapter 13

The *Kirkpatrick Business Partnership Model*^{SM}

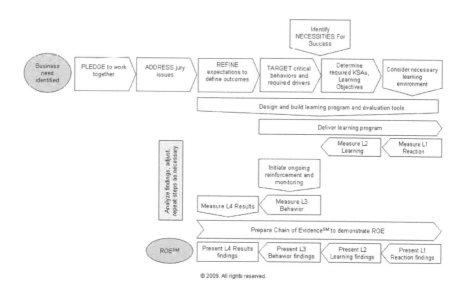

Here is the true, complete Kirkpatrick Business Partnership Model (KBPM^{SM}). While it contains many ideas the Kirkpatricks have been communicating over the last 50 years, we felt that a more complete illustration of the model would aid both learning professionals and their business partners to create more training value together.

Building Your Training Plan

The previous chapters have prepared you to follow each step of the model. Starting in the upper left corner of the model, a business need is identified. The KBPM starts with a formal connection between the business and learning, whereby a request is made to work towards resolving a business problem, or taking advantage of a market opportunity. This is where "the end is the beginning" comes into play. The first thing you want to do is clearly define from your stakeholders' perspective "what success will look like", and what result they are trying to accomplish.

The next step is pledging to work together. This involves making a good business case for partnership and generating commitment to a project in both business and training disciplines. This is often a much bigger challenge than the actual implementation of the science of the model itself. Finding an executive sponsor or champion can help to build the bridge between training and the business so you are able to move forward. The importance of this step was highlighted in chapter 10, Kirkpatrick Foundational Principle #3: Business Partnership is Necessary to Bring About Positive ROE.

The next step is to address jury issues. This is what we were talking about in chapter 9, when we discussed defining who is actually on your jury. We continued this conversation in chapter 12, when we discussed the fact that you should research your jury and find out what is important to them.

Now you perform the important task of "refining expectations to define outcomes". We talked about how to do this in chapter 8. It's critical to ensure you have moved past the surface request and into the true expectations of your business stakeholders. It is also important to make sure that what you plan to deliver is both measurable and achievable.

Following this is the often-forgotten yet imperative step of targeting critical behaviors and required organizational drivers. We hope we have emphatically imparted the importance of Level 3. This step is the foundation of your Level 3 action plan. This is the step that will differentiate you and define you from most other training professionals. This is where you lay the groundwork for the "magic" to happen. This is "the missing link", the connection between the training you perform and the results executives expect. Chapter 11, Kirkpatrick Foundational Principle #4: Value Must Be Created Before it Can Be Demonstrated explains why this is all so important.

Note "Necessities for Success" at the very top of the KBPM. Recall that these are cultural and systemic conditions that would either act as encouragers or discouragers of ultimate success *prior* to the initiative. Determining what these are for your initiative and creating the plan to address them was also covered in Chapter 11.

The next step gets back into familiar territory for training professionals. In fact, this is where most start the process today. Here you determine the required knowledge, skills, and abilities (KSAs) and define the learning objectives. The important point to remember here is that the learning objectives should directly map to the required on-the-job behaviors, and course content should be developed accordingly. This step is a critical place to keep your training program under control and prevent it from "growing" beyond what it needs to be to support the critical behaviors.

Then you consider the necessary learning environment. We feel this strongly ties to Level 1 Reaction. Think about what modality is going to work best to ensure that training participants are willing and able to perform critical behaviors when they leave the training class. Format Level 1 reaction sheets to measure these types of outcomes. Don't worry about if they liked the doughnuts, thought the instructor was funny, or appreciated being let go a few minutes early. These are not things that will support your Chain of Evidence nor impress business executives.

At this point if you have followed all of the steps, a solid training plan is built. Now you can start fleshing out the actual training program, or if you are lucky enough, pass the information to your instructional designers to do this for you. Remember to brief your entire training team on this process and make them a part of it. This may be a bit different than how training has been developed up until now in your organization, so make sure the process is known, understood, and accepted. Your good work in laying the foundation could be lost if your instructional designers don't build the training program with critical behaviors in mind.

Importantly (and often forgotten), this is also the time to determine the best way to measure each of the four levels, and build the tools and measurement plan you will use. Some of this work should already be done from when you refined expectations and defined outcomes. This is also a point to discuss with your instructional designers. They should build into the program information about how Level 3 and 4 will be reinforced, monitored, measured, and reported. Trainers and facilitators should explain this clearly to training participants so they are clear about what to expect. This is a good step towards success at Level 3.

Executing Your Training Plan

Next in the model comes "delivery learning program". This is also when formal evaluating begins with Level 1 and Level 2. Note that you may actually measure Level 2 before Level 1 during the course of the class. This is okay. The levels are not necessarily measured in order, nor does the order in which you measure them dictate what level you are actually measuring. What we mean by that is this: we have many well-intended training professionals forward to us what they believe to be Level 3 measurements. This is because they are administering the tool after the training session is complete. What we often find, however, is that the tool is a knowledge quiz, thereby making it a Level 2 Learning measurement. The nature of what is being measured, not the timing, determines what level you are measuring.

Some training professionals may be surprised to see that we are only about halfway through the KBPM at this point. This is a reminder that when the training class is complete, the training effort is just getting started.

We now move into new territory for many learning professionals with "initiate ongoing reinforcement and monitoring". This has everything to do with what happens *after* learning events, and deals with what we talked about under Kirkpatrick Foundational Principle #4: Value Must be Created Before it Can be Demonstrated. This step is Level 3: the supporting, monitoring and measuring of the critical behaviors, organizational drivers, and preliminary outcomes. While it is the job of the business to drive performance, it is the job of the training professional to make it as easy as possible for them to do so. This is also where training professionals can create not only tremendous value, but also goodwill through their support of Level 3 execution.

During this step is the time to partner with managers and supervisors who are responsible for ongoing coaching and reinforcement. Offer any assistance you can and follow up with them frequently. While this step in the process looks like one small box, it actually represents months or even years of effort.

Initiate Ongoing Reinforcement and Monitoring

This is where you will see 50 percent of learning effectiveness occur. It's where you can prevent 70 percent of potential learning failures if done properly. In short, we believe this one box is among the most critical in the entire model.

Note that on the left side of the model it says to "analyze findings, adjust, and repeat steps as necessary". This is just a reminder to continually check progress at each step and identify any problems that may require you to loop back and repeat a step. If you determine that conditions are limiting the ability of associates to learn or apply the information, now is the time to call attention to this and create a backup plan. There is no value in going through the entire process to find out at the end that intended results aren't achieved because of something that could have been corrected months earlier.

When the timing is appropriate, you can take your Level 3 and Level 4 measurements. There may be a span of time before it makes sense to do this. Depending upon the timing and complexity of the required on-the-job behaviors, you may not make your measurements until a few months after the training program. This is where a dashboard that tracks the behaviors and drivers can help you as an "early warning detection system". Don't wait until two months after training to find out that no one is performing the critical behaviors

Measuring and Reporting On Your Training Program

When you are satisfied with your preliminary findings at each of the levels, it's time to prepare your Chain of Evidence to demonstrate the ROE of your training program to the jury. Chapter 12 defines the types of evidence you want to collect and highlight based on the interests of your jury members.

Once the data and testimonials have been gathered and prepared, you are ready to make your final presentation to the jury. Note that you start with Level 1 and move sequentially through the four levels to create your value *story*. This means that you present your most important and compelling evidence last: the information about Levels 3 and 4.

Ultimately (and hopefully) this value-filled and evidence-based story will lead to a positive verdict: one where your stakeholders say that beyond a reasonable doubt, the overall learning initiative has successfully contributed to the intended results. In other words, successful ROE!

A Few Final Words on the KBPM

We opened this chapter by saying that the KBPM does not actually contain many new ideas that have not been previously published or explained by Don and Jim Kirkpatrick. Even with all that has been written here, we still believe this is true. We do believe, however, that much of this information has been lost over the years. Therefore we felt it appropriate, on the 50th anniversary of the first publishing of the 4 Levels, to reiterate the entire intent of the Kirkpatrick Model.

We hope you are now a disciple of business partnership, and see that the Kirkpatrick Model is more than a simple framework for summative training evaluation. It is truly a model for planning, executing, and measuring initiatives of any size. And we believe it to be as simply elegant as it was when it was unveiled in 1959.

We close the book with a request of you: to create your own personal action plan so that you can create your own legacy in the world of training and development, or whatever discipline you are passionate about pursuing.

Chapter 14

A Call to Action

You have just completed a brief history lesson. Most of us learned the old adage in school, "those who don't learn from history are doomed to repeat it". We thank you for taking the time to visit (or revisit) the four articles that started it all. More importantly, you have been given a tour of the modernized Kirkpatrick Business Partnership Model that better conveys the entire process and essence of what Don Kirkpatrick designed 50 years ago. And at a time like now when all expenditures are being carefully monitored, there is no better time to use the model to create, deliver, measure, and validate training with true business value.

There is also no better time to create a new standard within the learning industry. Allow us to explain with a personal story. We have a cement walk leading to the front door of our home. As Jim was walking up the path shortly after we were married, he noticed that the former owners depressed the footprints of (we assume) their small child, and carved his or her initials into the sidewalk. Upon seeing this 'legacy' left for all to see, Jim was somewhat envious that this former homeowner had been able to leave his or her mark. Jim wanted to do the same, but was too late. Obviously the cement had dried since 1995.

The good news is that *you* are not too late to leave your mark in the learning industry, as an individual or a team. During this time of economic challenge, when our industry is under fire, the good news is that business leaders – our jury members – are looking everywhere and anywhere for solutions to their incredible challenges. We have the unique opportunity to provide significant answers for them – and to carve out a new learning legacy, by becoming *true strategic business partners*. Fortunately, these economic times won't last forever. This creates a limited time frame and urgency for you to take action before the "cement" in the training and business world "dries".

Your Personal Action Plan

As a call to action, why don't you put the Kirkpatrick Model to personal use in the following way? We would like each of you to target a program coming up within the next year that could benefit from use of the entire KBPM. Choose something major enough that you can use what you have learned from reading this book.

To get started, consider your *own* views on the key questions at each of the 4 Levels. This will create a good starting point for when you first meet with your key business stakeholders to discuss the program.

Key Questions to Ask at Each Kirkpatrick Level

Level 4

- What will success look like?

- What evidence is needed?

- How will success be measured?

Level 3

- What critical behaviors will training graduates need to consistently perform on the job to bring about targeted outcomes?

- What are the required organizational drivers?

- What necessities for success exist within the organization?

Level 2

- What do training participants need to learn to be able to perform the required on-the-job behaviors?

Level 1

- What learning environment and methods are appropriate for what needs to be taught?

Thanks, Don, for a very useful 50 years. We duly appreciate the warning you gave us back in 1959, because indeed, the day of reckoning has arrived. It is up to all of us to heed your words and effectively apply what you and others have taught us. Thank you to all of you who have read this book and will help to shape the next 50 years.

RESOURCES

Glossary of Kirkpatrick Terms

AWACS (Airborne Warning and Control System): A U.S. Air Force aircraft that monitors battlefield conditions and activity. Parallels the Kirkpatrick approach to continually monitoring and reporting on Level 3 activity.

Borrowed metrics: Relevant Level 4 success outcomes that training professions obtain from business or human resource departments in order to complete a chain of evidence.

Business Partnership: Cooperative effort between the training department and other business and support units in the company.

Chain of Evidence^{SM}: Data, information, and testimonies at each of the four levels that when presented in sequence, act to demonstrate value obtained from a business partnership initiative.

Consumptive Metrics: Participant attendance, Level 1 and Level 2 data that attempt to show training value, but instead highlight the costs of training to the business.

Corporate Jury: The individual or group of business partners who ultimately judge the degree to which training efforts add value to the business in relation to their costs. This group subsequently controls or influences training department budgets, staffing, and future.

Critical Behaviors: The few, key behaviors that employees will have to consistently perform on the job in order to bring about targeted outcomes.

Dashboard: A graphic depiction of key metrics in a business partnership initiative that monitors and communicates progress towards business outcomes. Typically color-coded in green, yellow, and red.

Drivers / Required Drivers: Processes and systems that reinforce, monitor, encourage, or reward performance of critical behaviors on the job.

"The Great Divide": The significant gap that exists between Level 2 Learning and 3 Behavior, both in research correlation studies and actual practice.

Impact Metrics: Level 3 and Level 4 metrics, which constitute the most relevant measurements of training effectiveness to key business stakeholders.

"In order to what?": An important question asked during preliminary conversations defining the goals of a training initiative that helps move from training-centric to true business outcomes.

Key Business Stakeholder: A member of the jury that has a stake in the success outcomes of a training initiative, and ultimately judges the value of training relative to its costs.

Level 1 Reaction: To what degree participants react favorably to the learning event.

Level 2 Learning: To what degree participants acquire the intended knowledge, skills, and attitudes based on their participation in the learning event.

Level 3 Behavior: To what degree participants apply what they learned during the training when they are back on the job.

Level 4 Results: To what degree targeted outcomes occur as a result of the learning event(s) and subsequent reinforcement.

"The Missing Link": Another name for Level 3, because execution at this level is critical for maximizing Level 4 Results, yet neither training nor the business tends to take ownership for it.

Necessities for Success: Prerequisite items, events, conditions, or communications that help leverage success or head off problems before they reduce the impact of an initiative.

"Needles": The Level 4 metrics a training initiative is designed to move, that will effectively demonstrate training value to key business stakeholders. This refers to a needle on a dashboard indicating the current level of a critical measurement.

Return on Expectations^{SM} (ROE^{SM}): What a successful training initiative delivers to key business stakeholders demonstrating the degree to which their expectations have been satisfied.

Support and Accountability: The two forces that need to be balanced after training in order to drive critical behaviors (see *Transferring Learning to Behavior,* 2005).

"What will success look like?": The cornerstone question that helps convert generic stakeholder expectations to observable, measurable success outcomes, which subsequently become the Level 4 targets of ROE.

The Kirkpatrick Four Levels

Level 4: Results	To what degree targeted outcomes occur, as a result of the learning event(s) and subsequent reinforcement.
Level 3: Behavior	To what degree participants apply what they learned during training when they are back on the job.
Level 2: Learning	To what degree participants acquire the intended knowledge, skills, and attitudes based on their participation in the learning event.
Level 1: Reaction	To what degree participants react favorably to the learning event.

Chain of Evidence^{SM}

Level 1	Level 2	Level 3	Level 4
Reaction	Learning	Behavior	Results

Kirkpatrick Foundational Principles

Principle 1: The End is the Beginning

The end is the beginning highlights a necessary shift in thinking and doing in order for training professionals to overcome the barrier of getting a seat at the business table. Rather than continuing to start a change initiative with training and hope that it ultimately aligns with and leads to positive business results, training needs to follow and support business goals, beginning at the end – specific business expectations. Then and only then does training have a good chance to focus its efforts and make significant impact to the bottom line.

Principle 2: *Return on Expectations*[SM] is the Key to Success

It is our hope that *Return on Expectations (ROE*[SM]*)* will soon replace *Return on Investment* as the popular and true indicator of training effectiveness. ROE is powerful enough to showcase even the loftiest business and human resource goals, yet flexible enough to target individual business executive's own particular expectations for training. It is a living concept that all can relate to, as all employees, departments, and organizations have expectations to deliver on. While these expectations are important to negotiate, only when they are converted to measureable, observable indicators of success are they in the position to offer hope of ultimate, maximum impact.

Principle 3: Business Partnership is Necessary to Bring About Positive ROE

In order for business success to be maximized through training efforts, it will take more than training to do it. For years, there has existed the crippling myth that training events, in and of themselves, will lead to significant business results. Though many will resist a broader definition, research and actual practice clearly show that training and learning are only major cornerstones of ultimate business impact. In fact, a number of other factors must be put in place and actively executed in order for there to be a transfer of learning to on-the-job behavior, and ultimately to achieve targeted business and human resource results.

Principle 4: Create Value Before Trying to Demonstrate It

Another training industry misconception is that evaluation is to be used exclusively after training events to see if participants were engaged at Level 1, learned at Level 2, performed their jobs differently at Level 3, and contributed to positive business results at Level 4. In actuality, one of the most powerful uses of four level evaluation – and in this case, Level 3 – is to actually drive performance and results. With deliberate and persistent attention paid to Level 3 evaluation, coaching, reinforcement, role modeling, alignment of incentives, and accountability, training will be leveraged to actually create value. And that, then, sets the stage for us to confidently demonstrate programs that can significantly impact the bottom line.

Principle 5: Build and Present a Compelling *Chain of Evidence*[SM] to Your Corporate Jury

Once success outcomes have been achieved, and a determination of cause-and-effect ROE has been established through data and testimonies from each of the four levels, it is time to leverage that information by presenting it to your key business partners – and specifically, the sponsors of the particular initiative you are highlighting. We call this presenting a compelling *Chain of Evidence*[SM], much like an attorney does in his/her closing arguments to a jury. Primary purposes of making this passionate, powerful "story of value" are to show the power of the business partnership model in order to gain a seat at the business table, and to be seen and treated as a true strategic business partner.

Kirkpatrick Business Partnership Model^{SM}

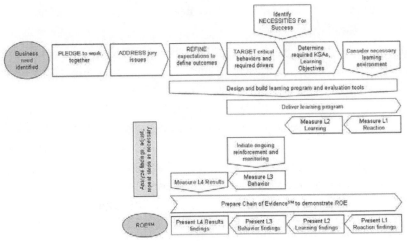

Kirkpatrick Business Partnership Model^{SM}

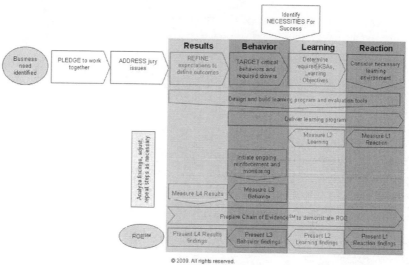

This version of the model shows the alignment of each step with the Kirkpatrick Four Levels.

About Kirkpatrick Partners

Kirkpatrickpartners.com

Kirkpatrick Partners, LLC was founded to help companies create, demonstrate, and measure true business value through their training and major initiatives.

Kirkpatrick Partners is proud to be directly owned and operated by Don and Wendy Kirkpatrick. When you work with us, you get the "genuine Kirkpatrick" materials.

Kirkpatrick Partners offers the following programs and services:

Seminars

- Kirkpatrick Four Level Evaluation Certification
- Training On Trial
- And many others!

Custom Training Events and Keynotes

We are happy to work with you to customize a message or program appropriate for your event or group.

Consulting

Get your training methodology custom made by the Kirkpatricks!

Register on our website to receive:

- Access to free articles, white papers, diagrams, and podcasts
- Subscription to our monthly e-newsletter

Kirkpatrickpartners.com

About Don Kirkpatrick, Ph.D.

Dr. Donald L. Kirkpatrick holds B.A., M.A., and Ph.D. degrees from the University of Wisconsin in Madison. His dissertation was "Evaluating a Human Relations Training Program for Supervisors".

At the Management Institute of the University of Wisconsin, Don taught managers at all levels the principles and techniques of many subjects including Coaching, Communication, Managing Time, Managing Change, Team Building, and Leadership.

In industry, Don served as Training Director for International Minerals and Chemical Corp. where he developed a Performance Appraisal Program. Later he served as Human Resources Manager of Bendix Products Aerospace Division.

Don is a past national president of the American Society For Training and Development (ASTD) where he received the Gordon Bliss and "Lifetime Achievement in Workplace Learning and Performance" awards. He is a member of Training Magazine's Hall Of Fame. In 2007, he received the "Lifetime Achievement Award" from the Asia HRD Congress.

Don is the author of seven Management Inventories and seven books including the 3rd edition of *Evaluating Training Programs: The Four Levels,* which has become the basis for evaluation all over the world. This book has been translated into Spanish, Polish, Turkish, and Chinese. His other books include: *Implementing the Four Levels, Transferring Learning to Behavior, Developing Employees Through Appraisal and Coaching* 2nd edition (2006);

How To Plan and Conduct Productive Meetings (2006); and *Managing Change Effectively* (2002).

Don is a regular speaker at national conferences of ASTD, IQPC, Nielsen (Training Magazine), and other professional and company conferences. He is a frequent speaker at ASTD chapters.

As a consultant, Don has presented programs to many U.S organizations and those in many foreign countries, including Singapore, Korea, Argentina, Brazil, Saudi Arabia, Malaysia, Greece, Netherlands, Spain, Australia, and India.

Don is the Board Chairman of South Asian Ministries, an active member of Gideons International, and a Senior Elder at Elmbrook Church in Brookfield, Wisconsin.

His hobbies include fishing, tennis, golf, big band and classical music, and directing church choirs.

For more information about Don and his work, visit kirkpatrickpartners.com and linkedin.com/in/donaldkirkpatrick.

Don can be contacted at don.kirkpatrick@kirkpatrickpartners.com.

About the Authors

James D. Kirkpatrick, Ph.D., is the Vice President of Global Training and Consulting for SMR USA.

Jim consults for Fortune 500 companies around the world including Harley-Davidson, Booz Allen Hamilton, L'Oreal, Clarian, Ingersoll Rand, Honda, the Royal Air Force, and GE Healthcare.

Jim is a masterful facilitator and conducts workshops on the Kirkpatrick Four Levels, the Kirkpatrick Business Partnership Model, and Training On Trial.

Prior to joining SMR USA in 2007, Jim was the director of the corporate university at First Indiana Bank. Since 1995, Jim has developed and managed a career development center, worked on senior strategic planning teams, and consulted with organizations all across the world in topics of evaluation, team building, coaching, and leadership, and conducted executive coaching.

Jim has co-written 3 books with his father, Don Kirkpatrick, the developer of the four levels. He has written a new book with his wife, Wendy, entitled, *Training on Trial,* (AMACOM Books, February 2010).

For more information about Jim and his work, please visit smr-usa.com and linkedin.com/in/kirkpatrickfourlevelevaluation.

Jim can be reached at jdkphd50@msn.com.

SMR USA

Wendy Kayser Kirkpatrick is the founder of Kirkpatrick Partners, LLC, a company dedicated to helping organizations become more effective through business partnership. She applies her skills as a certified instructional designer and expert presenter and facilitator to lead companies to measurable success.

Wendy's results orientation stems from her career beginnings in retailing; holding positions in merchandising, direct importing, and product development with Venture Stores and ShopKo Stores. From there she held marketing positions with Springs Industries and Rubbermaid. Most recently Wendy was a Training Manager for Hunter Douglas Window Fashions, managing the curriculum for 1500 sales and customer service representatives in North America.

Wendy and her husband, Jim, have written a second book called *Training On Trial* (AMACOM Books, February 2010). It provides training professionals practical ideas for how to partner with the business to produce measurable results.

Wendy is a national and local American Society of Training and Development (ASTD) member. She is serving on the ASTD 2010 International Conference and Expo Program Advisory Committee. She is active in her local ASTD chapter Communications committee. Wendy is also a faculty member for the American Management Association (AMA). Wendy speaks at events including the ASTD International Conference and Expo and the Training Magazine Learning Expo.

Wendy is originally from Madison, Wisconsin. She graduated from the University of Wisconsin with a B.S. in Retailing.

For more about Wendy, visit kirkpatrickpartners.com or linkedin.com/in/wkkirkpatrick. She can be reached at wendy.kirkpatrick@kirkpatrickpartners.com.

Bestselling Kirkpatrick Books

By Donald L. Kirkpatrick, PhD and James D. Kirkpatrick, PhD

"Don Kirkpatrick's name has long been synonymous with evaluation. This book provides, in one place, Don's best thinking on the subject.

I highly recommend it!"

> Bob Pike
> President
> Creative Training Techniques International, Inc.

"A must-read for every trainer and performance consultant.

Chock-full of real-life cases and implement-now ideas, Don and Jim have revisited the basics with a new twist – one you won't want to miss!"

> Elaine Biech
> Author of *Business of Consulting* and *Training for Dummies*

"Don and Jim's insights on management buy-in tactics and many practical examples of how to execute comprehensive level three and four evaluations are truly invaluable.

As no industry dynamics are exactly the same, I found the flexibility of the options/tools/resources around learning evaluations to be credible and comprehensive."

> Barbara Hewitt
> Executive Director
> MGM Grand University

Berrett-Koehler, Publishers, Inc.

Training On Trial

How Workplace Learning Must Reinvent Itself to Remain Relevant

By James D. Kirkpatrick, PhD and Wendy Kayser Kirkpatrick

Training on Trial is a real, pervasive situation in the world. This book explores how training has been charged with failing to make a significant, cost-effective impact on the bottom line using a courtroom analogy.

> Training has been charged with *failing to make a significant, cost-effective impact on the bottom line.*

Simply put, learning professionals and entire learning functions are in serious jeopardy if they cannot meet the needs of the business, and demonstrate that value to their business stakeholders. This also creates a tremendous opportunity for learning professionals who *are able to put the business partnership model into action.*

This book provides individual practitioners, training managers, CLOs, and business leaders with a practical, step-by-step approach to put the *Kirkpatrick Business Partnership Model*^SM into practice.

Highlights and best practices from Georgia-Pacific, Clarian Health and eight other organizations provide real-life examples of how learning has earned a seat at the boardroom table.

How Workplace Learning
Must Reinvent Itself
to Remain Relevant

TRAINING ON TRIAL

Jim D. Kirkpatrick, Ph.D
Wendy Kayser Kirkpatrick

AMACOM Books: February 2010

Made in the USA
Charleston, SC
08 August 2011